POPULAR CHRISTIANITY
ITS COWARDLY SERVICE
v. THE REAL WARFARE

*A SERIES OF LECTURES DELIVERED
IN PRINCES HALL, PICCADILLY*

CATHERINE MUMFORD BOOTH

This Edition is copyright of Diggory Press, 2007

British Library Cataloguing In Publication Data

A Record of This Publication is available
from the British Library

ISBN 1846855160
978-1-84685-516-0

This edition published 2007 by
Diggory Press, Three Rivers, Minions, Liskeard, Cornwall, PL14 5LE, UK
WWW.DIGGORYPRESS.COM

Printed on acid-free paper

PUBLISH YOUR BOOK
FROM ONLY £30 OR US$50!
With our self-publishing imprint,
Exposure Publishing!
SEE WWW.DIGGORYPRESS.COM

PREFACE

IN committing these addresses to the press, I would like to say to my readers that although for months after their delivery I was continually pressed to publish them by many of my hearers, I steadily refused, chiefly because I feared that in cold type they might produce an impression of censoriousness, which was not possible when, as I believe, assisted by the Spirit of God, I dealt with my hearers face to face on these burning topics.

During my late illness I became deeply convinced that it was my duty to let these utterances, such as they are, go forth irrespective of consequences, in the hope of reaching a greater number of persons similarly circumstanced with those to whom they were originally spoken, many of whom professed to have received great personal blessing, with increased light and power for usefulness.

Having come to this conclusion, I submitted the MSS. to my friend Commissioner Railton, who not only strongly urged me to publish them, but favoured me with some most valuable suggestions and emendations.

May He whose kingdom and glory alone I seek bless every reader with grace to receive whatever truth he may find in these pages applicable to himself in the love of it.

CATHERINE BOOTH.   *LONDON, July, 1887.*

LECTURE I

THE CHRISTS OF THE NINETEENTH CENTURY COMPARED WITH THE CHRIST OF GOD

The Christs of the Nineteenth Century

I SUPPOSE there will be no division of opinion in my audience as to the fact that humanity needs a Christ,--that everywhere and in all ages, men and women have been, and are still, conscious of a strife with evil; not merely physical evil represented by thorns and thistles, but with moral evil--evil in thought, in intention, in action, both in themselves and in those around them. This consciousness of wrong has thrust upon men the realization of their need of help from some extraneous power, or being. In all generations men have seemed to feel that without such help there must be a perishing.

This sense of need has been forced upon men, first, by the failure of their own repeated efforts to help and save themselves.

Secondly, by their observation of such fruitless efforts in others.

What man or woman who has thought at all, who has not stood on the edge of this human whirlpool, and watched the struggling multitudes as they have risen and sunk, striving and struggling by resolutions, by the embracing of new theories, by taking of pledges, and making new departures, to escape from the evil of their own natures and to save themselves? Who has watched the struggle without realizing the need that some Almighty independent arm should be stretched out to deliver and to save? Who can read history or contemplate the experience of humanity at the present time, without realizing that it needs a Saviour, whatever idea may be entertained as to the kind of Saviour required?

Further, this sense of need is the outcome of the filial instinct born in every human soul, which cries out in the hour of distress or danger to an Almighty Father,--a God,--a friend somewhere in the universe, able to help and to deliver. This instinct is at the bottom of all religions, and more or less embodied in all their formulas, from that of the untutored savage up to the profoundest philosopher the world has ever produced. Perhaps the cry of humanity, destitute of a Divine revelation, could not be better summed up than in the following words of Plato, who, speaking of the soul and its destiny, says:--

"It appears to me that to know them clearly in the present life is either impossible or very difficult; on the other hand, not to test what has been said of them in every possible way, not to investigate the whole matter and exhaust upon it every effort, is the part of a very weak man. For we ought in respect to these things, either to learn from others how they stand, or to discover them for ourselves, or, if both these things are impossible, then taking the best of human reasonings, that which appears the best supported, and embarking on that, as one who risks himself on a raft--so to sail through life--unless one could be carried more safely, or with less risk, on a secret conveyance, or some Divine Logos."

In this confession, and in that of many others similar, we see, as it were, a mighty soul prying through the gates of life, striving to fathom the mysteries of being and to unlock the unknown future,--in fact, crying out for a Christ, a Divine Word, or Logos, a something or somebody who should guide him, taking him up where human reason and philosophy failed him. It is also worthy of note that it has always been the highest type of man in all ages who has cried out most persistently for an extraneous deliverer. The more conscious of his own powers and the higher in his aspirations man has become, the more vehemently has he sought, outside of himself, for light and deliverance. Surely this universal cry of humanity, in all its phases and throughout all ages, betrays a great want, casting its shadows before-- the cry of the creature responding to the purpose of the Creator to send a **SAVIOUR** able to save to the uttermost of man's necessity. The great realized want of humanity was a deliverer who could take away its sense of guilt, enlighten its ignorance, and energise it for the practice of all goodness and truth,--a being who could not only stand without and legislate as to what men were to do, but who could come within and empower them to do it. Heathen philosophies and ancient religions could say, "Love thy neighbor," but they could none of them inspire the man to do it, much less enable him to love his enemy--none of them even aspired to command that. That was beyond humanity. Here, then, was the great need of a power to come inside and rectify the wrong, making the spring right, so that its outcome might be right.

Further, I want to remark that in the Bible a Christ is offered that meets this need. This is the great distinguishing boast of our faith--the only religion on the face of the earth in which the idea of a Christ has ever been conceived. The Bible offers this Christ. The golden chimes of great joy that rang out on the day when He was heralded by the angels, were to be glad tidings to all people of a Saviour which was Christ the Lord, a mighty deliverer, able to cope with man's inability, with the disadvantages of his circumstances, and the consequences of his fall. Now we contend that this Christ of the Bible, the Christ who appeared in Judea 1800 years ago, is now abroad in the earth just as much as He was then, and that He presents to humanity all that it needs; that He is indeed, as He represented Himself to be, the Bread of Life come down from heaven, the Light, and the Life, and the Strength of man, meeting this cry of his soul which has been going up to God for generations. Here I stand and make my boast, that the Christ of God, my Christ, the Christ of the Salvation Army, does meet this crying need of the soul, does fill this aching void, and does become to man that which God sets Him forth as being in this book. Guilty humanity He promises to pardon, and He does pardon. Ignorant humanity (with respect to God and the things of God) He promises to enlighten, and He does enlighten it. Degraded, sunken, impure humanity (in the very essence of its being) He promises to purify, and He does purify it. We make our boast of this Christ, and we say He is able to save to the uttermost, and that He does this now as much as ever He has done in the 1800 years that are past,--that He is a real, living, present Saviour to those who really receive and put their trust in Him.

I know that many may answer, "This is not the Christ that is generally presented in the preaching and teaching of this age, or that is generally professed and believed in by the Christians of this age; neither do we see such results as you depict in their characters or lives." Granted. The sceptics and the infidels say: "We do not see these results, and therefore we do not believe in your Christ." And I say, looking at the question from their standpoint, I should feel just as they do, because they have a right to have these results proved to them. It is useless telling of wonderful things having transpired a long time ago and a long distance away. They say, Show them now; show us the men in whom this change is wrought, and then we will believe that this Christ always does these things. I say Amen, and that because they do not see these signs in the popular Christianity of this day, therefore they reject its Christ, and there is great excuse for them,--not such excuse as will justify them at the bar of God, because they ought to have found out Christ for themselves,--nevertheless, an excuse to themselves and to their fellow-men.

I say, I grant that this is not the Christ exhibited in these days.

I will now try to give to you, as I perceive them, those modern representations of Christ which, instead of drawing all men unto Him, have driven the great mass away from Him, and disgusted many of the ablest minds with the whole system of existing Christianity.

False Christs

The first imaginary Christ of this age seems to be a sort of **religious myth or good angel**--a being of the imagination who lived in the long distance, and who does very well to preach, write, and sing about, or to make pictures about, with which to adorn people's dwellings--a kind of religious Julius Cæsar, who did wonderful things ages ago, and who is somehow or other going to benefit in the future those who intellectually believe in Him now; but as to helping man in his present need, guilt, bondage, or agony, they never even pretend that He does anything of the kind. This Christ makes no difference in **them** or their **lives**; they live precisely as their neighbors do, only that they profess to believe in this Christ while their neighbors do not.

Now this is not the Christ represented in the New Testament. The Christ of God was a real veritable person, who walked about, and taught, and communicated with men; who helped and saved them from their evil appetites and passions, and who promised to keep on doing so to the end of the world; who called His followers to come out from the evil and sin of the world to follow Him, carrying His cross, obeying His words, and consecrating themselves to the same purposes for which He lived and died; seeking always to overcome evil with good, and to breast the swelling tide of human passion and opposition with meekness, patience, and love; promising to be in them an Almighty Divine presence, renovating and renewing the whole man, and empowering them to walk in His footsteps.

I am afraid there are thousands who sit in our churches and chapels and hear the modern Christ descanted on, who, if asked their idea of Christ, would be utterly at a loss to give it. They have no definite conception of what His name or being means. They would not like to say whether He is in heaven or on earth. If asked whether He had done anything for them personally, they cannot tell; the most they say is that they hope so, or that they hope He will do something some day. He is to them a mere idea.

Another false but very common view of Christ in these days is that He is a sort of **Divine make-weight**. You will hear people say, when spoken to about their souls, "Yes, I know I am very weak and sinful, but I am doing the best I can, and Jesus is my Saviour; He will make up what I lack." In these instances there is not even the recognition of the necessity of pardon, much less of the power of Christ to renew the soul in righteousness, and to fit it for the holy employments and companionships of heaven. This Christ is simply dragged at the tail, not only of human effort but of human failure, and offered, as it were, in the arms of an impudent presumption, as a make up in the scale of human deserts. And yet how many thousands of church and chapel going people, it is to be feared, are deluded by supposing that this imaginary Christ will meet the needs of their souls before the judgment bar of God.

To others this imaginary Christ is only a superior human being, **a beautiful example**--the most beautiful the world has ever seen; not Divine, yet the nearest to our conception of the Divine which even they think possible, but only human still. This Christ is held up as the embodiment of all that is noble, true, self-sacrificing and holy--an example of what we are to be, but supplying no power by which to conform ourselves to the model.

I frequently find that the people who make so much ado about the example of Christ are the furthest from following it. They say it is not intended to be followed literally. But how else can you imitate any one? How can an example be followed figuratively? Alas! The admirers of this human Christ make it sadly manifest in their lives and experience that humanity needs not only a model, but an inspiring presence to restore its lost balance, energise its feeble faculties, and rekindle its spiritual aspirations. Conceiving only of a human model, the paralysed soul finds no higher source of strength than its own desires and resolutions, and after the oft-repeated experiment at self-deliverance, sinks at length overwhelmed with a sense of failure and despair. It is not in man or angel, however sublime, to free the human soul from its fetters of realized guilt, or to empower it for the reconquest of that Eden of righteousness and peace from which the avenging angel of justice once expelled it. A human Christ is only a phantom of the imagination, an *ignis fatuus*.

Another modern representation of the Christ is that of a **substitutionary Saviour**,--not in the sense of atonement merely, but in the way of obedience. This Christ is held up as embodying in Himself the sum and substance of the sinner's salvation, needing only to be believed in, that is, accepted by the mind as the atoning Sacrifice, and trusted in as securing for the sinner all the benefits involved in His death, without respect to any inwrought change in the sinner himself.

This Christ is held up as a justification and protection in sin, not as a deliverer from sin. Men and women are assured that no harm can overtake them if they believe in this Christ, whatever may be the state of their hearts, or however they may, in their actions, outrage the laws of righteousness and truth.

In other words, men are taught that Christ obeyed the law for them, not only as necessary to the efficacy of His atonement for their justification, but that He has placed His obedience in the stead of, or as a substitution for, the sinner's own obedience or sanctification, which in effect is like saying, Though you may be untrue, Christ is your truth; though you may be unclean, Christ is your chastity; though you may be dishonest, Christ is your honesty; though you may be insincere, Christ is your sincerity.

The outcome of such a faith only produces outwardly the whited sepulchres of profession, while within are rottenness and dead men's bones. The Christ of God never undertook to perform any such offices for His people, but He did undertake to make them "**new creatures**," and thus to enable them to perform them for themselves. He never undertook to be true instead of me, but to make me true to the very core of my soul. He never undertook to make me pass for pure, either to God or man, but to enable me to **be** pure. He never undertook to make me pass for honest and sincere, but to renew me in the spirit of my mind so that I could not help but be both, as the result of the operation of His Spirit within me. He never undertook to love God instead of my doing so with "all my heart and mind and soul and strength," but He came on purpose to empower and inspire me to do this. The idea of a substitutionary Christ accepted as an outward covering or refuge, instead of the power of "an endless life," is a cheat of the devil, and has been the ruin of thousands of souls. I fear this view of Christ, so persistently preached in the present day, encourages thousands in a false hope while they are living in sin, and consequently under the curse not only of a broken law, but of a Saviour denied and abjured. Let me ask you, my hearers, what sort of a Christ is yours? have you a Christ who **saves you**, who renews your heart, who enables you to live in obedience to God, or are you looking to this outside and imaginary Christ to do your obeying for you?

Another false idea of Christ, entertained, I fear, by multitudes of sincere souls, is that of **a Divine condemnation**.

This class of people seem to think that they ought to spend all their lives bewailing and bemoaning their sins, and are for ever crying out, "Oh, wretched man that I am," "Christ have mercy on us, miserable sinners"; and they go on crying this every day of their lives. They forget that He of whom Moses and the prophets did write, **is come**. They forget that the deliverer is here--that pardon is offered, and that He is ready to witness it and fill their souls with peace and joy. If Christ be only for condemnation, what are these poor souls advantaged by His coming? what has He done more than the law did, for them? The law made them realize their bondage, writhe under a sense of their sins, and set them longing after freedom and deliverance. It was their schoolmaster (or should have been) to bring them to Christ--Christ, the Son, who was to make them free; but alas! in this case He is made a much harder schoolmaster than the law itself, for these poor souls get no deliverance, no peace, no joy, or power. They are always piping Paul's bewailing notes, in which he personified a convicted sinner, struggling under the fetters of condemnation. But they never get into his triumphant notes, where he declares, "there is now no condemnation."

This false view of Christ has led to most of the idolatries, penances, and lacerations of Catholicism.

The exhibition of a Christ too unsympathetic and implacable to be approached without a second intercessor--a far-off, austere judge, rather than a pitying, pardoning Saviour--has kept millions of poor souls in bondage all their lives. I must say, however, that I have more sympathy with such souls, because they **are** sincere, and earnest, and willing to deny themselves, in order to find the right way, than with those who thoughtlessly take refuge under any of the false representations of Christ to which we have referred. It is to be feared, however, that the same spirit of worldliness which has so largely destroyed the power of Protestantism, has, to a great extent, extinguished this groping after Christ in the Catholic Church. I confess that I cannot see sufficient cause for congratulations such as are common in Protestant circles over the decadence of Popery, seeing that everybody knows that it is not in consequence of a growth of real heavenly light, but only the further spread of a careless, godless, take-it-easy spirit, putting out the earnest desire for purification which formerly led to so much self-sacrifice in the church of Rome. There can be no doubt that it is through the loss of this true spirit of devotion that the evils which have crept into that Church have so completely over-shadowed the good, and prevented the multiplication of St. Bernards and others who got through the self-despair into the purest light and joy. Still, there are many earnest souls left, who continue to cry over their sins as though no deliverer had come. The Christ of God came not to bring condemnation but pardon, peace, and gladness to every penitent sinner on the face of the earth. I heard, the other day, a story which beautifully illustrates this: A poor Catholic woman, who had been in bondage all her life to a sense of guilt, and had earnestly sought by all the methods prescribed by her Church, especially by devotion to the Virgin Mary, to find peace and deliverance, when on her death-bed was brought into contact with one who had in reality found the Christ of God, and who was enabled to show to this poor trembling soul the sufficiency of His sacrifice, and His willingness to pardon and to purify. Through the influence of the Spirit of God which accompanied this exhibition of the true Christ, she was enabled to rest her soul on Him, and immediately entered into rest. Shortly afterwards her priest presented himself at her bedside, when she accosted him with the words, "Oh, you are too late, too late, I have found a better Priest than you, and He has absolved me. I am happy, happy, happy!"

The Christ of God is not a condemnatory Christ, but a pitying, pardoning Saviour, calling to His bosom the weary and heavy laden in all ages.

Another of these false views of Christ is that which presents Him as **a future deliverer, without being a present Saviour**.

It is to be feared that thousands are looking to Him to save them from the consequences of sin--that is, hell,--who continue to commit sin; they utterly misunderstand the aim and work of the Christ of God. They do not see that He came not merely to bring men to heaven, but to bring them back into harmony with His Father; they look upon the atonement as a sort of make-shift plan by which they are to enter heaven, leaving their characters unchanged on earth. They forget that sin is a far greater evil in the Divine estimation than hell; they do not see that sin is the primal evil. If there were no sin there need be no hell. God only proposed to save people from the consequences of sin by saving them from the sin itself; and this is the great distinguishing work of Christ--to **save His people from their sins!**

The Christ of God

Now I deny that any of the representations of Christ to which I have referred are the Bible representations of the Christ of God, or that they meet the need of the soul of man. They are for the most part made to meet the ideas of a modern worldly Christianity.

Men have made up their minds that they can possess and enjoy all they can get of this world in common with their fellow-men, and yet get to heaven at last. They have made up their minds that it is all nonsense about following the Christ,--becoming a laughing stock to the world, which He made Himself every day He lived,--and setting themselves to live a holy life, which He said if they did not they were none of His; all this they have abandoned as an impossibility, and yet, not content without a religion, and finding it impossible to look into the future without a hope of some sort, they have manufactured a Christ to meet their views, and spun endless theories to match the state of their hearts. The worst of all, however, is that a great many of the teachers of Christianity have adopted these theories, and spend their whole lives in misrepresenting the Christ of the gospel.

Now let me try to put before you what I conceive to be the true representation of the Christ of God. We say that He meets the whole world's need--that He comes to it walking on the waves of its difficulties, sins, and sorrows, and says, "I am the Bread of Life; take Me, appropriate Me, live by Me, and you will live for ever. I will resuscitate and pardon, cleanse and energise you; I am the Christ, the Saviour of the world." This is the Divine "Word," or deliverer, which philosophers have longed for, and stretched out their dying hands to embrace--which all the heathen world have, more or less, groped after in some dim figure.

First: **The Christ of God is Divine.**

We admit the incarnation was a mystery, looked at from a human standpoint, but no greater mystery than many other incarnations taking place all around us, and because a mystery, none the less a necessity. Humanity must have a deliverer **able to save**, and no less than an Almighty deliverer was equal to the task. Here, all merely human deliverers, all philosophers and teachers of the world, had failed, because they could only teach, they could not **renew**. They could set up a standard, enunciate a doctrine, but they could not remove man's inability, or endue him with power to reach it. Here even the law of God failed, and that which was ordained to life wrought death. Here was the sunken rock, the bitter maddening failure of all systems and deliverers,--they failed to **rectify the heart**; they could not give a new life or impart another spirit.

We saw at the outset that man needed some being outside of himself, above him, and yet able to understand and pity him in his utmost guilt, misery, and helplessness--able to inspire in him with **a new life**, to impart light, love, strength, and endurance, and to do this always and everywhere, in every hour of darkness, temptation, and danger. Humanity needed an exhibition of God, not merely to be told about Him, but to **see** Him; not merely to know that He was an Almighty Creator, able to crush him, but that He is a pitiful Father, yearning and waiting to save him. God's expedient for showing this to man was to come in the flesh. Can the wisest modern philosopher or the most benevolent philanthropist conceive a better? How otherwise could God have revealed Himself to fallen man? Since the fall man has proved himself incapable of seeing or knowing God; he has ever been afraid of the heavenly, running away even from an angel; and when only hearing a voice and seeing the smoke which hid the divinity, he exceedingly feared and quaked, and begged not to hear that voice again. Truly, no man as he is by nature can see God and live. Seeing then, that God desired that man should see Him--that is, know Him--and live, notwithstanding his fall, He promised a Saviour, who should reveal Him in all the holiness and benevolence of His character, and in His plenitude of power to save!

Here the Christ of God presents Himself, claiming to be this Divine Saviour. An objector may ask for proof of His Divinity. This would be far too great a subject to go into now, but we may glance at two or three considerations, which are quite sufficient, unless, indeed, Christ were an imposter.

First, those who reject His Divinity say He is the nearest to the Divine of anything we can conceive. They say He is the best of the good of our race--even infidels cannot find fault with His character; they all bow down before the spotless purity, the beneficence and moral beauty of Jesus Christ. All schools grant this. Then, taking my stand here, I say that this perfect being **claimed to be Divine**, and He claimed it so unmistakably and persistently, that if you take it out of His teachings, you reduce them to a jumble of inconsistencies. His Divinity is the central fact around which all His doctrines and teaching revolve, so that if this be extinguished, they become like a system of astronomy without the sun, dark, conflicting, and inconsistent. Read the Gospels and illiminate for yourselves all His assumptions of Divinity, and then see what you can make of His teaching.

Secondly, these assumptions were understood and resented by the people to whom He spoke, and they surely were the best judges as to what He meant. If they had mistaken His meaning, He was bound, merely as a man of honour, to explain Himself, but He never did; so when the Jews said, "Whom makes Thou Thyself," or, "This man maketh himself equal with God," He did not demur nor retract, but repeated, "I came forth from the Father, and I go to the Father." This was the one intolerable point in His teaching, which the Jews, who owned no plurality in gods, could not endure; that any other being should be one with their Jehovah was to them insufferable, and for this they ultimately crucified Him. "What further need have we," said the high priest, "of witnesses? Behold, now ye have heard His blasphemy."

Then, if He were so near an approach to perfection as even infidels admit, how was it that He allowed such an impression of His teachings to go abroad, if He were not Divine? How could He say, "If ye believe not that I am He, ye shall die in your sins," if He had not known Himself to be the Christ of God?

Thirdly, His character supported His assumptions. For 1800 years millions of the best of the human race have accepted these assumptions without being shocked by them. If He be not Divine, how comes it to be that the greatest of human intellects, the sincerest of human souls, and the most aroused and anxious of human consciences, have ventured their all upon this Divine word, and have seen nothing contradictory between His claims and the actual character which He sustained in the world; whereas, imagine the very holiest and best who ever trod our earth putting forth such assumptions, and how would they sound! Suppose Moses, who had talked with God in the burning bush, or Isaiah, whose tongue was touched with the live coal from off the altar, or Daniel, the man greatly beloved, to whom the angel Gabriel was sent again and again, or the apostle of the Gentiles, who was admitted into the third heaven, or the beloved apostle John,--suppose any of these men saying, "I am from above, ye are from beneath," "I am not of this world," "If ye believe not I am He, ye shall die in your sins." "I came forth from the Father, and am come into the world." Again, "I leave the world and go to the Father"; and in His prayer on the eve of His agony, "The glory which I had with the Father before the world was," and again, in answer to Philip's request, "Show us the Father,"--"Have I been so long time with you, and yet hast thou not known Me? he that hath seen me hath seen the Father;" "believest thou not that I am in the Father, and the Father in Me?"

And not only does He claim this oneness of essence with the Father, but also that omniscience which enables Him not only to be with His people but to dwell in them, as shown in His answer to the question of Judas, when he asked how it was that He would manifest Himself to His own people and not to the world. Jesus answered, "If a man love Me, he will keep My words: and My Father will love him, and we will come unto him, and make our abode with him."

Think of any creature--a David, a Paul, a John, daring to claim from himself this omniscience. If this Christ were not Divine, then there is no alternative; he was altogether an imposter and a deceiver.

From such a conclusion, however, even infidels and blasphemers shrink, and therefore we must be allowed to hold to our faith in our Divine Redeemer--our Immanuel, "God with us." I may ask here, if there is one of my hearers whose consciousness does not tell him that he needs a Divine Saviour? Would any less than an Almighty, omniscient, infinite deliverer meet the needs of your souls? If so, you must feel much better and stronger, and more able to help yourselves than I do. "Great is the mystery of godliness: God was manifest in the flesh, justified in the Spirit, seen of angels, preached unto the Gentiles, believed on in the world, received up into glory."

But take this mystery out of Christianity, and the whole system utterly collapses. Without a Divine Christ Christianity sinks into a mere system of philosophy, and becomes as powerless for the renovation and salvation of mankind as any of the philosophies which

~ Popular Christianity ~

have preceded it. But no, our Joshua has come, our Deliverer is here; He is come, and is now literally fulfilling His promise to abide, "I and my Father will come unto you, and make our abode with you." He comes now in the flesh of His true saints, just as really as He came first in the body prepared for Him, and He comes for the same purpose, to renew and to save; He is knocking at the doors of your hearts even now, through my feeble words, and will come into your hearts if you will let Him. As He came walking over the sea of Galilee to the men and women of His own day, He comes now to you, walking over the storm raised by your appetites, your inordinate desires, passions, and sins--a storm only just gathering, waxing worse and worse, and which, unless allayed, will grow to eternal thundering, lightnings, and billows; but He is able to allay it, He offers to pronounce "Peace, be still," and end this tempest of your soul for ever. Will you let Him?

Second: The Christ of God offered Himself as a **sacrifice for the sin of man.**

The Divine law had been broken; the interests of the universe demanded that its righteousness should be maintained, therefore its penalty must be endured by the transgressor, or, in lieu of this, such compensation must be rendered as would satisfy the claims of justice, and render it expedient for God to pardon the guilty. We will not attempt to go into the various theories respecting the atonement; it is enough for us to know that Christ made such a sacrifice as rendered it possible for God to be just, and yet to pardon the sinner. His sacrifice is never represented in the Bible as having purchased or begotten the love of the Father, but only as having opened a channel through which that love could flow out to His rebellious and prodigal children. The doctrine of the New Testament on this point is not that "God so hated the world that His own Son was compelled to die in order to appease His vengeance," as we fear has been too often represented, but that "God so **LOVED** the world, the He **gave** His only begotten Son."

As Christ represented His union with the Father as perfect and entire on every point and in every particular of His humiliation, so He represents it as equally complete with respect to the sufficiency and vicarious character of His death. "**THEREFORE** doth My Father love Me, because I lay down My life, that I might take it again. No man taketh it from Me, but I lay it down of Myself. I have power to lay it down, and I have power to take it again."

He so shows that in baring His won heart to the sword of justice, He was equally with the Father interested in the maintenance of the dignity of the law, and equally inspired with boundless and quenchless love for its transgressors.

There has been a great deal of empty talk as to the needlessness of a vicarious sacrifice, and many contend that the Father's love flows out to all His creatures independently of any such intervention; but, setting aside the requirements of the Divine law altogether, I venture to assert that there has never been a human conscience awakened in any measure to the deserts of sin, which has not instinctively felt the need of such a sacrifice. In thousands of instances, even with the strongest representations of the infinity, value, and efficacy of the atonement, it requires the utmost effort to get the trembling soul to rest its hopes on the merit of even this Divine sacrifice, and all history proves that in no other way have sinful consciences **ever been able to find rest**.

Third: The Christ of God is an **accepted sacrifice**.

This has been attested by His resurrection from the dead. God has declared to the three worlds, of angels, men, and devils, that justice is satisfied, and that henceforth no guilty son or daughter of Adam need despair of His mercy and salvation--the accepted sacrifice for all men, and we know not for what other beings. How far-reaching its benefits are we cannot tell,--perhaps to distant planets and suns; any way, they reach to you and to me.

In view of this sacrifice God waits to pardon your guilt, cleanse your pollution, transform your character, and hallow, and beautify, and utilize your life. You have no longer any excuse for groaning under the dominion of sin. He calls you forth from the tomb of your depravity; He calls you out of the dungeon of your guilt, and offers you a full and free acquittal, with all the resources necessary for a new life of righteousness, peace, and joy in the Holy Ghost.

Fourth: The Christ of God is an **embodiment of His Father's righteousness**.

He will only administer the benefits of His sacrifice in accordance with the Divine standard of right. He will do no violence either to the government of God or the nature of man. Although love was the supreme ingredient of His character, yet we hear no words of an indiscriminate charity dropping from His lips, no excuse of sin, no palliation of the guilt of enlightened transgressors of His Father's forbearance. He hated iniquity as supremely as He loved righteousness. The great end and aim of His coming was the regeneration and restoration of man to the mind and will of God; hence He confirmed the first and greatest commandment, "Thou shalt love the Lord thy God with all thy heart, and with all thy soul, and with all thy mind, and with all thy strength."

Fifth: The Christ of God claims to be the **Sovereign of all whom He saves**. He tells us, if men keep not His words--do not obey Him--they are none of His; and He claims absolute inward and outward obedience to His precepts every hour of every day of all the life of every one who professes to be His subject.

My friends, have you accepted Christ? Do you know Him as your Divine Almighty Deliverer from the strength and power of sin? Have you cast your weary soul on Him as your sacrifice, claiming freedom from the condemnation of the past? Have you the witness of His Spirit that this sacrifice has been accepted by God on your behalf, and does the answering cry, "Abba, Father," go up from your soul? Are you living in the regeneration of His Spirit, carefully seeking to fulfill all righteousness, commending your every act to Him in faithful obedience? Does He reign over you as the sovereign of your heart and life, and do you hold everything you possess,--yourself, your children, your property, your time, your influence, your reputation, your life, your death,--subservient to His will and interests? If so, happy are you, and your example before men and your influence in the world will be worthy of the professed followers of the "Christ of God."

LECTURE II

A MOCK SALVATION AND A REAL DELIVERANCE FROM SIN

I SUPPOSE that most of those present this afternoon are aware that the subject is "A mock salvation in comparison with Christ's salvation"--deliverance from sin. As I said last week with respect to a Christian, so I may say this week with respect to salvation, that there will be no difference of opinion as to the need of our race for a salvation of some sort. This must be too patent to need argument,--that our world is disordered, disjointed, morally diseased, and that it needs some sort of regenerating, rectifying process, if society is not to be disorganised by its own corruptions, or sunk for ever in the hell of its iniquities. Every man knows this to his own hurt. All men have a personal consciousness of being wrong, whether they believe in a Divine revelation or not; nay, whether they believe in God or not. I do not think I have spoken to more than half a dozen people in my life-- and I have spoken, I suppose, to some thousands of different classes-- who have maintained that they were right. Even infidels, when you face them with the question, "Are you right? are you living according to the dictates of your judgment and conscience?" dare not say they are. The universal cry of our poor humanity is, "Oh, wretched man that I am!" whether it be looking for any Divine deliverance or not. Men everywhere know that they are not living according to their own conceptions of right, and therefore they have a sense of self-condemnation; and this asserts itself in spite of their arguments and excuses. It is of no avail to the soul tormented with a sense of guilt to say, "The woman tempted me," or "I was under the pressure of great fear, or shame, or dread"; this is no real palliation. Hence the universal fear to face the future, the disinclination to think about God, the predisposition to blind the eyes to the proofs of His existence, and to harden the heart against His claims. Truly conscience makes cowards of us all until cleansed from dead works, purified and restored to the throne of the soul.

Further: not only do all men feel this sense of wrong in themselves, but they expect wrong in others. Even parents anticipate

~ *Popular Christianity* ~

and provide for it in their children. Every parent knows that there is a tendency in his children to go astray from the very first moment of accountability. He knows that there is in his child a tendency to speak lies as soon as it can speak at all, that there is a tendency to perverse tempers and wicked passions. Hence wise parents universally recognise, whether they make any pretensions to Christianity or not, the necessity of family government and careful training in order to check, counteract, or eradicate, as the case may be, these tendencies to evil; and thus they acknowledge the necessity for a certain kind of salvation in their children, and they recognise also this fact, that if they do not attempt to work out this salvation, the children will bring them to wreck and ruin. A child left to itself brings its mother to shame; we know that sadly too well.

There is the same recognition of the need of a salvation amongst men of the world. Every intelligent business man goes on the assumption that he has to encounter wrong in the hearts and conduct of his neighbors; in fact, the world takes it as a sign of intelligence that a business man goes on this assumption, and would call him a fool if he did not. He knows that he is beset on all hands by those who will over-reach, cheat, and ruin him for anything that they care, if they can promote their own interests by so doing. Hence the necessity for a kind of legal salvation, in the form of agreements and bonds, between man and man.

I hear a good deal about this in connection with our negotiations for buildings, which we are carrying on every day. When proprietors and agents have made certain offers or promises, the General says, "Have you got it in black and white?" and if the answer is "No," then he says, "What is the use of it?" Alas! We know only too well that it is of no use; and I am sorry to say that this is as true of many professing Christians as of worldly men. Why is this? Because a man's word is nothing in the great majority of instances. Hence the necessity for lawyers, magistrates, and judges; and even these have to be tied down by law, and watched and supervised, lest even the judges should turn traitors to justice, and, for the sake of bribes or party considerations, sell the interests of those whom they ought to protect. Here again is the recognition of the necessity for a **salvation** for these very people who are placed as guardians of public justice and the administrators of the law. This salvation many of them specially require when dealing with the poor Salvation Army. By the way, it is a curious fact that such is the impression produced by the Army, that again and again politicians on both sides of the Atlantic have laughingly represented various combinations of statesmen as "salvation armies." How often do politicians in different lands represent their countries as being, in some particular verging on ruin, and needing a "salvation"? What is this but a great public confession, made by those best capable of judging, that whole nations are misled? for in these days of popular government most people have to be cajoled into voting, to their own injury. Moreover, we have it from the highest public authority that nation after nation goes astray on questions vitally affecting their highest good; and it is commonly asserted that they are deliberately led astray by men who care only for their own interests, and so contrive to delude their fellow-men wholesale.

It is evident that but for these temporal salvations to which I have alluded, the world would be unendurable for us to live in. You know this. You know that it is not safe for a man to trust his brother; "for there is none upright among men, ... they hunt every man his brother with a net."

Here, then, is the patent, palpable necessity for a salvation. Now, the question is, What sort of salvation meets the necessities of the case? What kind of a salvation does God our Maker, who knows what He meant us to be at the first, and who knows perfectly what we have become through sin,--what kind of a salvation does **HE** propose for humanity?

I answer, He proposes a salvation that deals with and removes the **cause** of all this wrong and woe.

Our Saviour, in Matthew xv. 19, goes to the root of the evil when He says: "For out of the heart proceed evil thoughts, murders, adulteries, fornications, thefts, false witness, blasphemies." And the apostle also, in Galatians v. 19: "Now the works of the flesh are manifest, which are these; adultery, fornication, uncleanliness, lasciviousness, idolatry, witchcraft, hatred, variance, emulations, wrath, strife, seditions, heresies, envyings, murders, drunkenness, revellings, and such like: of the which I tell you before, as I have also told you in time past, that they which do such things shall not inherit the kingdom of God." Whether you believe in the revelation or not, you will agree with the fact that these are the works coming everywhere from the evil heart of man; there is no getting away from that. Then I say that God proposes to deal with and remove the **cause**--

the wrong state of the heart. If all men's hearts could be set right today, we should need no more temporal, legal, or political salvations; no more lawyers, police, magistrates, or judges; for a salvation that renews the heart would render all these unnecessary.

God's plan of salvation in dealing with the internal malady embraces all its external consequences.

It is evident, then, that any salvation which does **not** deal with this leprosy of evil in the heart is a mockery.

As I showed last week that there are, alas, many false, delusive, disappointing christs; so I have to show this week that there are many make-believe, mock salvations, which only deceive, disappoint, and damn those who trust in them. As I walk about the world, and as I look at professing Christians, my soul crys: O God, make haste to help us to raise up a holy people, in order to show the world what salvation really means, for they do not know. They are utterly befogged and bewildered, and I do not wonder.

We will now look at a few of these mock salvations, for they are legion. First, I want to premise that anything, no matter how valuable in itself, **which is put in the place of something for which it is no substitute is a mockery.** For instance, here is a stone, very valuable in its right place--especially if it be in one of the shops in Oxford Street; but offered to a starving man in a desert it is a mockery; because, valuable as it is, the man cannot eat it, and he will die notwithstanding that stone, worth a thousand pounds, lies at his feet, because there is no substitute for bread.

Now, there are endless substitutions for salvation. It has been the devil's plan from the beginning to make imitations of God's best things. Perhaps it is a necessity that evil must try its power upon all God's creatures as it did upon Adam; we do not know. Probably there was no other way or working out the transcendant value and beauty of goodness that by allowing it to come in contact with evil; if this be so, of course it applies to God's remedies for sin; anyway, the devil has done his worst on these. God's plan of salvation is at present in this crucible. The devil is trying to circumvent it, and his favourite plan for doing this is by forging plenty of mockeries.

We will look at these under four divisions,--**Salvations of theory; salvations of ceremony; salvations of mere belief**, and **the salvation of unbelief.** First, let us look at salvations of theory. You see it matters very little what kind of a theory a man has; if it be substituted for salvation it becomes a mockery,--a true theory no less than a false one.

The devil no doubt has a correct theory; I fancy that he is a much better theologian than many Christians, but he remains the old serpent still.

It is doubtless better to have right opinions that wrong ones, but the best opinions will not save man. I am afraid there is a great deal of preaching that amounts to a mere putting of the different theories about salvation, instead of persuading men to come to Christ and be saved.

The main idea of much of the preaching of this day seems to be that of teaching people--instructing them,--which too often results in hardening their hearts, and finding them an easier way down to perdition than they would have found without it. Unfortunately a man feels more comfortable when he has been to a place of worship and heard a fine theory **about** salvation, than he would if he had not been, although he may be no nearer being saved. All preaching, Sunday School teaching, tract writing and distribution, or any other instrumentally which has not for its end the immediate salvation of the people, only leads them to trust in mere teaching, which is a mockery. It is like giving a dissertation on the relative value of a vegetarian and an animal diet to a man dying of hunger. What good will your dissertation do unless you get the man to eat of the food about which you are descanting. And, unless your teaching induces men and women to eat of the Bread of life for themselves, it is a mockery! And yet how few preachers or teachers, how few religious workers have this as their main idea--the end at which they aim. You can see the want of it in the way they fail to bring men to Christ there and then. How my heart has ached over this aimless, pointless preaching, I could not express. Perhaps, when I have had the rare opportunity of a Sunday's rest, I have gone to some near place of worship, hoping to be refreshed or stimulated, and to see sinners saved, or at least convicted, but alas! I could only weep as I listened to dissertations on some creed or doctrine which had probably been believed and approved by everybody present since they were children, while the poor empty **souls** were left starving for want. I have felt like saying to the minister, "My brother, if you have nothing better than this to offer, let us have a prayer meeting and get something direct from the great Father himself, without your intervention." Would to God there were more preachers in the fix of a Baptist minister in a town where we are just now having

~ Popular Christianity ~

a glorious work, who has been so stirred up and awakened to his responsibilities, that, on a recent occasion when he had read his text, he broke down, weeping, which had more effect than all the sermons he had preached during the years he had been in that town. His people wept too, and many of them got converted over again. I wish that a few thousands of the ministers of this kingdom could be brought to a similar state of mind before next Sunday; what a commotion there would be in the land, and what a stir in hell, ah, and in the heavens too!

But further, I want you to note that any theory which teaches people to rest in a mere **intellectual belief in the Scriptures**, or any doctrines therein, while their souls are left in bondage to sin, is a mockery, and it is one of the most popular mockeries of this day.

Oh, Christians say, "Scatter the word," and they have been scattering the word for generations, spending thousands of pounds over it, and I could enlighten them as to what becomes of the word in thousands of instances when it **is** scattered. We always get wrong when we depart from God's way, and this is not His way. It is not written that "it pleased God to save by the distribution of Testaments, those who believe," but it pleased God to save by the foolishness of preaching--by the living testimony of living men--by those who embody the word in their experience and lives, and then go and speak it in the power of the Spirit to others. This is the sort of preaching God has commanded. Study and love the written word as much as you like, but remember that the letter killeth, and that you will never save men by merely giving them the letter; and I point to the miserable results of this plan as proof of the truth of what I say.

I fear the giving away of texts and tracts has proved a most successful stratagem of Satan's for enabling Christians to salve their consciences in resisting the Spirit's urgings to a bold, straight-forward testimony for Christ. It is so much easier politely to hand one of these silent messengers, than to make a determined onslaught on the sinner's conscience, and to try to persuade him there and then to flee from the wrath to come. Not only is it easier for the Christian, but it is also much more endurable for the unsaved; consequently he is willing to make a compromise, and in order to escape from straight, plain, personal dealing, he will pocket a tract, laughing in his sleeve at the cowardice of the giver; because he knows perfectly well that Christians, to be consistent with what they profess, ought to make a desperate effort for the immediate salvation of every unsaved man and woman with whom they come in contact. The world wants living epistles who will live, weep, act, suffer, and, if need be, die before the people. The testimony of such witnesses will prove a living word indeed, sharper than any two-edged sword.

I say that the knowledge of and belief in this whole Bible, from beginning to end, if substituted for actual, personal salvation, will prove as great a mockery as any other sentimental belief.

No mere intellectual beliefs can save men, because right opinions do not make right hearts. Alas, we all know the little practical effect opinions have on character. Look around you. Do you know any man who is not a thorough intellectual believer in chastity being better for a man, or a woman, in the end, than uncleanness? Is there any wicked, profligate young man, whom if you could take him aside and talk fairly to him, would not tell you that he believed that chastity was the best for a man, and yet you have only to look at him to see that he is a sepulchre of uncleanness and debauchery. What avails his intellectual belief in chastity while he is the slave of his lusts? What better is the man who believes in chastity and sins, than a man who does not believe in chastity and sins? As a French infidel, answering a caviller against holiness, said the other day, "You believe and sin, I do not believe and sin: where is the difference? It seems to me I am the better of the two." Exactly, for however true or grand a man's beliefs, of what use are they if he does not act them out? "Can faith save him?" Nay, verily, but **such** a faith **can** damn him.

Further, any theory which **leads men to suppose that they are safe** without being actually saved is the most dreadful of all.

Such a theory adds an intellectual opiate to the deceit of the heart, and prevents the truth from troubling the conscience. Now, the only use of appealing to the understandings of the unregenerate, is, that through their understandings you may get at their hearts, but if Satan has "blinded their minds" by some intellectual opiate, there is no chance. The understanding is darkened, the conscience seared, and the soul paralysed. These are the worst people in the world to preach to; when I had to preach to them, how I groaned many a time for a congregation of heathen. I have found such now in the Salvation Army--I mean, a people whose understandings are not darkened by these false theories and intellectual conceits. One **can** get the light in through their heads into their hearts, and this is the reason of our success with them; and is not this the reason why the publicans and the

~ Popular Christianity ~

harlots have always gone into the kingdom of God, while the natural children of the kingdom have been left out?

A man is either saved or not; the **fact** is independent of his theory, and it is of comparatively little consequence what his theory may be if he be saved. Hence many savages and Catholics have rejoiced in a consciousness of pardon, while many evangelicals have never known it. A man is either under the dominion of sin, or else he is delivered from it. If he is under the dominion of sin, what an awful theory is that which makes him believe he is saved. Could the devil have invented a more damning theory than that? And yet, alas! alas! he allures millions to destruction through it, who otherwise would take alarm and being to seek salvation. He says to all the qualms of conscience and the pangs of remorse, "You are all right, you believe this or the other, your faith is orthodox, you are safe," frequently quoting separated or mutilated texts to back up his lying insinuations, such as--"By faith ye are saved;" "he that believeth shall be saved;" "you are complete in Him," etc. This latter phrase has come to express, in numbers of instances, the most utter ruin to which the human soul can be brought. "Complete in Christ"! complete without any true repentance, without any offering of the heart, without the slightest change inward or outward, "complete in Him," while living without Him, and having to conscious connection with Him whatever; complete without losing one evil feature of the godless life, without receiving one grace of any kind, without doing or suffering anything, except perhaps a whispered "I believe;" complete all in a minute, since somebody pointed to a text with which perhaps the poor victim had been familiar all his life. Complete in Christ with a gnawing consciousness at the heart that it is as sinful, as empty, as powerless, and as joyless as ever; complete as a poor corpse would be complete, if painted and dressed in the clothes of a living man! May God save you from any such mock salvation as this.

Further, any theory that leads men to trust in **general confessions and prayers** for salvation, is a mockery.

How many thousands of people every Sunday confess to being "miserable sinners," and cry to God to have mercy upon them, without the slightest appreciation of the meaning of the words they utter. They feel better and safer because of these confessions and prayers, whereas their prayers remove them further, rather than bring them nearer, to any real salvation. What is the use of prayer that produces no effect, that brings no answer? Here is a mother whose boy is condemned to die: the father goes to the Queen to beg for his life. When he returns, the mother says, "Well, have you succeeded?" He answers, "I have put up my petition before the Queen." "Well, but what is the answer?" "Oh, you must not expect a direct answer: I have no answer, not have I any reason to believe that I shall get one, but I have put up my petition." The mother would say, "That is a delusion; I want to know whether my boy is going to be released; I cannot sleep in my bed till I know what the answer is!" Now, I say, people who go on petitioning God for years together, never concerning themselves about the answer, or even expecting one, show that they are utterly insincere, and consequently obnoxious to God, and yet there are thousands of such people, who go to and fro to our churches and chapels every Sunday like a door on its hinges. They say, "O Lord, have mercy upon us, miserable sinners," but they have no real desire for His mercy, no recognition even of the necessity for the forgiveness of sins, no concern about living to please Him, no idea of what repentance or salvation really means! Is it not manifest that such hypocritical confessions and prayers render those who engage in them more impervious to the truth, and more oblivious to any true idea of salvation, than they would be without them? God says such prayers are an abomination to Him. There is only one kind of prayer from an unconverted soul which is acceptable to God, and that is the prayer that is wrung out of the heart by anguish for sin.

Further, another mock salvation is presented in the shape of **ceremonies and sacraments**. These were only intended as outward signs of an inward spiritual reality, whereas men are taught that by going through them or partaking of them, they are to be saved. Amongst these may be classes Baptism, the last Supper, and the ceremonials of ancient or modern Churches.

Oh, the thousands of souls who are resting their hopes of salvation on the fact that they have been baptized, not only such as believe in the palpable delusion of baptismal regeneration, but amongst ordinary church and chapel going people. As I look at our Army congregations in Rinks, Theatres, and other similar places, and note the signs of sin, debauchery, and crime on many of their faces, I say to myself, I suppose all these people have been baptized; but I do not think there are many thieves, or harlots, or drunkards, or openly immoral people who claim baptismal regeneration. Thank God! It is only genteel sinners who can bring themselves to believe in such a palpable sham, and yet, if baptism possesses any efficacy, it should be as effective in the one class of sinners as in the other.

What an inveterate tendency there is in the human heart to trust in outward forms, instead of seeking the inward grace! And where this is the case, what a hinderance, rather than help, have these forms proved to the growth, nay, to the very existence, of that spiritual life which constitutes the real and only force of Christian experience!

It is a calamity deeply to be deplored that men should thus put the form in the place of the power, but they have always been doing so. It is only another species of that idolatry which has prevailed from the foundation of the world. Take, for instance, the brazen serpent. All are familiar with the story of that miraculous intervention of Jehovah on behalf of the Israelites dying from the poisonous bites of the fiery flying serpents, sent as a punishment for their rebellious murmuring. God directed Moses to exhibit a brazen serpent on a pole, and to proclaim to the bitten multitudes that all who would look to it should be healed. Thousands looked, and as they looked were cured. In memory of that wonderful deliverance, and doubtless also as an emblem of the coming Saviour, that serpent was preserved; but when, in the years that followed, the people who came to attach undue value to the ceremony of viewing it,--burning incense before it, with idolatrous worship,--Hezekiah, jealous for the honour of Him whom this form was only intended to shadow forth, called it "Nehustan," *i.e.*, a piece of brass, which it really was, breaking it in pieces and casting it away with the trees of the groves and the altars of the high places which the people had desecrated by idolatry. Now, we have nothing to say against forms; but they are only, as it were, the bodies in which spiritual ideas and purposes are manifested, and without **LIFE** they are useless, and worse than useless.

When forms are exalted, and idolized, and trusted in, no matter how beautiful in themselves, or how Divine in their origin, they become "Nehustan," as a piece of brass, or a piece of bread, or a bowl of water. As the apostle said of circumcision, when the Jews had put it in the place of righteousness, "Neither is that circumcision which is outward in the flesh. Circumcision is that of the heart, in the spirit, and not in the letter; whose praise is not of men, but of God." And although originally ordained by God, he says again: "Circumcision is nothing, and uncircumcision is nothing, but the keeping of the commandments of God."

We feel persuaded that if Paul were here now, and could see the deadly consequences which have arisen from the idolatrous regard given to what are called the Sacraments of the Supper and of Baptism, he would say precisely the same with respect to them; for even if Jesus Christ intended them to be permanent institutions (against which there are very strong arguments, as put forth by many most devoted and intelligent Christians ever since the days of the apostles, amongst whom are the "Friends" of our own time), such is the awful abuse to which these ceremonies have been subjected, that we feel sure Paul would say Baptism is nothing, and the ceremony of the Lord's Supper is nothing, apart from keeping the commandments of God, especially that great and all-comprehensive commandment, "Thou shalt love the Lord thy God with all thy heart, and mind, and soul, and strength, and thy neighbour as thyself."

Christians often say to me, when I put this view before them, "Ah, but you have no authority to remit the Supper, because the Lord said we were to take it in remembrance of Him till He come!" I answer that He left the taking of it at all perfectly discretional; and as to its continuance, that entirely depends on which coming He alluded to. "Friends," and many others of the most spiritual and deeply taught Christians of all times, have believed that He then referred, as in so many other places which are generally misunderstood, to His coming at the end of the Jewish dispensation. Any way, our Lord, who had long before said to the woman of Samaria, "The hour cometh when ye shall neither in this mountain nor yet at Jerusalem (in any special sense) worship the Father.... But the hour cometh, and now is, when the true worshippers shall worship the Father in spirit and in truth," anywhere and everywhere, could not have intended to teach that God could be more acceptably or profitably worshipped through any particular form or ceremony than without such form or ceremony, and especially if there were weighty reasons on the other side for rejecting it!! Neither is it credible to a spiritually enlightened mind that He who said, "If a man love Me, he will keep My words, and My Father will love him, and we (I and My Father) will come unto him, and make our **abode** with him," could have intended to teach that through the earthly medium of bread and wine His people were to **remember** Him on whom their thoughts were to be constantly concentrated, or to commune with Him in any special sense above that in which they were to commune with Him always and everywhere. The water which Jesus gives, and to which alone He attaches any importance, is that which is "in us a well of water springing up into everlasting life"; and the wine which He values and promises to drink with us in His Father's kingdom, is that wine of the kingdom which is righteousness, and **peace, and joy** in the Holy Ghost.

Friends, do you partake of **these** sacraments? If not, rivers of earthly water, vineyards of wine, will avail you nothing; they will be as "Nehustan."

If we were to have any binding forms in the new and spiritual kingdom in which all forms were to find fulfilment, it seems to me that there is a great deal more ground for insisting on washing of one another's feet than for either of those already referred to; and in this we can see a great practical lesson on the human side which our Lord actually laid down. How comes it, I wonder, that many of those who regard the former with such sanctimonious reverence, can utterly, and without scruple, set aside the latter? I fear that human pride and priestly assumption must be held largely responsible.

Further, nothing is more evident to all who have any acquaintance with the history of Christianity, than that the undue value set upon these ceremonies has been one of the greatest hindrances to the extension of Christianity. Again and again have its valiant warriors paused in their triumphal progress, and turned aside from the battle with the great forces of evil, to quarrel amongst themselves concerning these mere externals.

When I was in Ireland, some of the oldest and most experienced Christians who took part in that great revival some twenty-five years ago told me that a great proportion of the results of that wonderful work of God were lost, in consequences of a controversy about water baptism. Do you wonder that we of the Salvation Army shrink from the possibility of such a sacrifice of the greater to the less--especially when we are backed up by the great apostle of us Gentiles thanking God that he baptized none of this early converts, and for the very same reason, namely, because they were making the ceremony a cause of controversy!

Further, what can be the value of imitating the marchings and vestments and songs of the ancient Jewish Church? We are not accepted in the beloved Jews, and if these ceremonies had become, as God said they were, a stink in His nostrils because of the backsliding unbelief and hardness of heart of His ancient people, how much greater must the offence of them be when adopted by impenitent, infidel, and rebellious Gentiles. Neither can it be any less repugnant to the mind of

God, that spiritually uncircumcised Philistines should dare to put their hands to His ark, by anticipating the signs, ordinances, and alleluias of the Church triumphant. What have such people to do with the songs of martyrs and confessors, or with the alleluias of the angel bands who stand before the Lord in His temple? "Rebellion is as the sin of witchcraft, and stubbornness is as iniquity and idolatry." And yet what multitudes who are hardening their hearts and stiffening their necks every day against the claims of God and of His truth, dare to bow down to what they call the table of the Lord and unite in what they believe to be the songs of saints and angels. The first qualification for participating in any spiritual exercises or ceremonies, is the **renewal of the heart** by the Holy Ghost. If you could have the very same ceremonial which they have in heaven, with angels as your ministers, unless you had the spirit of it within, it would profit you nothing. "Though I speak with the tongues of men and of angels, and have not the love of God, I am nothing." And our Lord said, with respect to some of His hearers, "Then shall ye begin to say, We have eaten and drunk in Thy presence, and Thou hast taught in our streets. But He shall say, I tell you, I know you not whence ye are; depart from Me, all ye workers of iniquity"; showing that even where Christ Himself was the preacher, if the heart remained under the bondage of sin and in the gall of bitterness, the hearers would only inherit greater condemnation, and sink into a deeper hell.

I must not omit to say a word here on the salvation of unbelief, notwithstanding that I purpose to enlarge on it at a future time. The most astounding theory of all the false theories about salvation, and also the latest novelty propagated, alas, from Christian pulpits and through the Christian press, as well from avowedly infidel platforms, is that man is to be ultimately saved from his errors and iniquities, and especially from all trouble concerning them, by a simple negation. He is to dismiss from his mind all the creeds, all idea of any precise revelation, and to get light from any natural earthly source he can, especially from the modern lights, who are responsible for this new theory. He is to throw his mind back as far as is possible towards heathenism, nay, further back than those enlightened heathen philosophers to whom I referred in my first lecture, for he must on no account even sigh after anything supernatural or Divine. He is to believe in himself and in humanity; especially the future of humanity-- seeing that there are so many ugly facts about its present. Thus he will have no more difficulties, sighings, or cryings!

He is to put away everything unpleasant and unsightly as far as he can, even if it professes to be the word of God, and possessing his soul (no, I beg your pardon, his mind) in patience, to wait and hope till the law of evolution has transformed our poor sin-stricken and groaning earth into a heathen paradise!

What a striking reproduction is this modern revelation, only in a new fashion, of the words of fools thousands of years ago, who used to say, "How doth God know? and is there knowledge in the Most High?" and who "consider not that they do evil."

Truly we may say of all these theories, ceremonies, prayers, faiths, and unbeliefs, which are palmed on man as substitutes for salvation from sin, Vanity of vanities, cruel mockeries, making destruction doubly sure.

Poor humanity still cries out, "Who will show us any good?" Miserable comforters are ye all, leaving us still on the dunghill, covered with wounds, bruises, and putrefying sores. **WHAT SHALL WE DO TO BE SAVED?**

Deliverance from Sin

Let us now consider the character of that salvation proposed by God for our race. The salvation of God embraces deliverance, restoration, preservation, and glorification.

Of course the mere idea of salvation supposes some enemy, bondage, disease, or danger; there can be no salvation where there is nothing to be saved from. All the saviours raised by God for Israel during their national existence were actual deliverers of their people from their enemies, otherwise they could not have been saviors. Moses, Joshua, Gideon, Nehemiah, and many others, were real deliverers of their people; they delivered from the outward consequences of sin; but the great distinguishing feature of our Joshua is that He delivers His people from their spiritual enemies, and from the power of sin itself. Where there is no deliverance there can be no salvation. What a mockery and a delusion it is for a man to profess to be saved, while he is groaning under the power of his spiritual enemies. If you are under the domination of sin, you are yet an utter stranger to the salvation of God.

First: Salvation implies **restoration**.

Salvation to a man who is sick means restoration to health; to man who is drowning, restoration to dry land; to am man dying, restoration to life; to a man on the verge of bankruptcy it means liquidation of his debts, and restoration to solvency.

The common sense of mankind has prevented any theoretical deliverances or mock salvations for these temporal maladies and destructions, but our great adversary, who lieth in wait to deceive, has succeeded, as we have already seen, in deluding men and women, as to the reality of Salvation when applied to the soul. But the salvation of God is no less real and practical for the soul than any of these temporal salvations are for the body or the circumstances.

What is man's disease? Sin, badness, falseness, spiritual death. Salvation means restoration to goodness, to truth, to spiritual life, and to God. It means deliverance from inward evil, and renewal of the heart in righteousness and true holiness. It means the right adjustment of the faculties of the soul, bringing it into harmony with the laws of its own being, with the law of God, and with the rightful claims of its fellow beings. In short, it means being **PUT RIGHT** in all its relations for time and for eternity.

Second: Salvation implies **preservation**.

In order to the well-being and happiness of a being who has been saved from any disaster or death, there must be a provision for his continuance in a state of health or safety. It would be a small mercy to save a man from drowning, if he were under the cruel necessity of throwing himself into the water again to-morrow; and equally small would be the mercy pardoning a sinner, and restoring him to a sense of peace and purity, if no provision had been made for his continuance in such a state of salvation. The salvation of God contemplates all the weaknesses and necessities of fallen human nature; hence the Christ of God becomes "the author of eternal salvation to all them that obey Him." He not only restores, but He promises to dwell **in** His people as the power of an endless life, enabling them to purify their hearts by faith, to love God with all their souls and strength, and to offer themselves as living sacrifices, holy and acceptable in His sight. He promises to empower them to resist the devil, to keep themselves unspotted from the world, and to fight manfully under the banner of His cross till death.

Do you ask for living witnesses of such a salvation? Thank God, there are thousands who can testify that they have passed from darkness to light, that they have been delivered out of the hands of all their enemies, and are now enabled to serve God, walking before Him in righteousness and holiness day by day--thousands, not of genteel, refined, religiously trained people, such as most of you here to-day, but from amongst the most ignorant, neglected, besotted, and openly wicked of earth's populations. They stand forward, an exceeding great army of witnesses to the reality of the salvation of God, and to the power of His Christ to deliver, to restore, to purify, and to keep all those who really receive and obey Him.

Third: The Salvation of God embraces also **glorification**.

How do we know? Well, first, reasoning from analogy, and seeing that the great change wrought in true saints is in the **soul**, and that it manifests itself in spiritual and heavenly instincts, dispositions, and aspirations, which do not find their full development or satisfaction in this life, we conclude that there is a future and more congenial sphere for such development and satisfaction.

Secondly, we have the most satisfactory evidence which mortals can give, of future glorification in the fact that many are glorified before our eyes in death. Amidst the humiliation, pains, and agonies of physical dissolution, we see the soul emerging from the wreck of its physical environment, triumphing over him hath the power of death, and in regal majesty pluming its wings for its final flight, and in view of such a victory, human reason, no less than Divine revelation, declares: "Death is swallowed up in victory."

Are there any here who want salvation? Come and try our Saviour Lord. He can cure your disease, extract the poison out of your heart, and make you **new creatures**! We testify that He has done this for some of us on this platform; whereas we once were the children of wrath, because the children of sin, even as others, now He has made us the children of God and of light, enabling us to seek those things that are above.

Consistently with our profession, we consecrate ourselves, our whole being, our children, influence, time, life, and, if need be, death, to the pressing of this salvation on the attention and acceptance of our fellow-men. We make all things bow down before this unbending resolution, to seek and to save the lost.

LECTURE III

SHAM COMPASSION AND THE DYING LOVE OF CHRIST

The Sham Compassion

BENEVOLENCE has come somewhat into fashion of late. It has become the correct things to do the slums, since the Prince of Wales did them; and this general idea of caring in some way or degree for the poor and wretched has extended itself even into the region of creeds, so that we have now many schemes for the salvation of mankind without a real Saviour.

Do not misunderstand me. I have no objection--nay, I rejoice in any real good being done for anybody, much more for the poor and suffering-- I have no objection that a large society of intelligent Christians should take up so noble an object as that of caring for stray dogs, providing it does not interfere with caring for stray babies! I desire not to find fault with what is good, but to point out the evil which, to my mind, so largely diminishes the satisfaction one would otherwise feel in much benevolent effort being put forth around us. As I said at the beginning, the most precious stone given instead of bread is useless to a starving man.

Surely nobody ever cared for poor suffering humanity so much as Jesus Christ. He gladly put forth His mighty power for the healing and feeding of the body, and He laid it down most distinctly that all who were true to Him must love the poor and give up their all for them in the same practical way in which He did; but all this real brotherhood did not prevent His keeping the great truths of **salvation ever to the front**, and applying them as relentlessly to the poor as to the rich, and *vice versâ*.

But now in the name of Christ we are asked to believe either that the truest way to carry out His intentions is to ignore men's souls and care only for their bodies, or else to join with this sort of material salvation some theory that will practically get rid of all serious soul-need.

The First Scheme

of salvation without a Christ provides for attention to all the needs of this body, ignoring the soul.

This system has not only become more popular in many Christian circles than any of Christ's teachings, but some of its advocates actually go so far as to place it in favourable contrast with any spiritual work whatsoever, thus plainly intimating that hose who really have the spirit of Christ show it better by devotion to these so-called practical ends than by what are assumed to be the less practical efforts which have regard to the world to come. This religion of bodily compassion may almost be said to have many sects devoted to it, each having their own favourite theory.

First, we have the **educationalists**.

These almost abandon the existing generation, but are confident of the results of their labours upon the coming one, such results being conveniently remote. But whether in connection with week-day or Sunday schools, this plan has had at least the trial of one generation, with extremely bad results so far as we can judge. What a mockery of mankind to suppose or to teach that mere information can satisfy its wants, when the more information men get, the more clearly we see the reign of evil in the world, and the hopelessness of attaining to righteousness, so far human power is concerned. Yet, strange to say, the efforts of an enormous proportion of the mission agencies at work are directly devoted to education, and the ablest heathen in the world to-day are those who have been carefully instructed in missionary institutions, and have used their education to obtain higher positions and greater influence in the world, with which they now the better withstand the gospel of Christ.

Many of the more sensible Christians, perceiving how little ordinary education can do for the toiling masses, devote their attention to mechanical education, hoping to raise the position and prospects of the working classes by teaching them how to put a better finish on their daily tasks, although it is notorious that the cleverest of workmen are frequently the greatest drunkards and the most miserable of men.

Second on this list, for the regeneration of society, we have the **house-builders**.

These are afflicted, and rightly so, with the overcrowded condition of the working-class dwellings, and consider that all will be well when the people are better housed, shutting their eyes to the condition of multitudes who may be seen to-day living in the greatest sin and misery in well-built modern dwellings. Certainly it is a shameful scandal on those Christian landlords who keep their tenants in buildings unfit for dogs; but, after all, not so much more shameful than the conduct of those who, although aroused to the frightful condition of the masses, deliberately attempt their improvement on the same principles as if they were cattle, mainly by means of buildings which pay a liberal interest. No one could possibly be more thankful than I should to see the compassion which has of late found such loud expression in words, embodied in some practical scheme for the provision of comfortable, wholesome houses for the poor, at such rental as they could comfortably pay; but to provide this, with land under our present iniquitous system, will require a benevolence willing to "lend, hoping for nothing again."

Thirdly: Next comes the **total abstinence plan** for the salvation of the people.

Amongst those who devote themselves to this sphere of labour there are some of whom I would speak with the greatest respect, namely, those who perceive that in all these outward things there is no remedy without some radical internal change. The majority, however, observing that drink has more than anything else contributed to the degradation of the people, concentrate their efforts upon their deliverance from this one evil--unquestionably a great temporal good-- but we have only to look across the Channel to see abundant evidence that the people may be almost clear of drunkenness without being, for that reason, and **nearer to God** or true happiness. To soberise without **saving** can only be compared to the action of a set of people who should with heroic effort drag drowning men ashore, and then leave them lying all unconscious within reach of the waves.

Fourthly: Another scheme of temporal salvation may be represented as **rescuing work**.

There are benevolent efforts of many kinds put forth for the rescue of various classes of fallen or endangered people from their several perils, without a thought of placing them in spiritual safety. I am not speaking with the least desire to depreciate any of these efforts; but what I would point out is, that while Christ held up for condemnation the priest who haughtily passed by the poor victim, He no less held up to condemnation the Levite who deliberately looked at his necessities and yet passed on. I desire to give every credit for true kindly feeling on behalf of the fallen or suffering; but it seems to me unaccountable that intelligent beings should look upon any form of human ruin without realizing that something must be done **within**, as well as without, in order to produce any lasting change for the better.

Fifthly: Another plan of temporal salvation is the **providing for needy children**.

This is one of the most favourite hobbies of benevolent people, and properly so, if it were only carried out in the right way. But how astounding, that people professing to revere and follow **Christ** should be capable of entertaining any schemes which undertake the guardianship of children, and yet which ignores their spiritual necessities, which trains and teaches them how to get on in the world **without God**. Alas! I know from personal experience and actual contact with some of the children turned out of orphan asylums of high reputation in Christian circles, that, so far as any real living acquaintances with the things of God, or any practical carrying out of the teachings of Jesus Christ, are concerned, they might as well have been brought up amongst infidels; and I am by no means alone in this opinion. I have reason to believe, that in many such instances, nothing would be more highly resented than any attempt to make such children realize the willingness and sufficiency of a personal living Saviour to renew their hearts and to enable them to walk in obedience to His will, and to keep themselves "unspotted from the world." Dry conventional dogmas and ceremonies constitute the only notion that thousands of such children have of the religion of Jesus Christ; and no wonder, considering the specimens they have had exhibited to them in the conduct of many of those whom their poor little lives and hearts have been committed. I have many times said what I here deliberately repeat, that if I were dying and leaving a family of helpless children, I would leave it as my last request that they might be divided--one here, and another there--amongst any poor, but really godly, families who would receive them, rather than they should be got into the most highly trumpetted orphanage with which I am acquainted; for I should infinitely prefer that their bodies should lack necessary food and attention, rather than that their poor little hearts and souls should be crushed and famished for want of love, both human and Divine. Children brought up without love are like plants brought up without the sun. I would suggest to some of you ladies who may be on committees, or who might possibly get on to them, that you would be doing God and humanity good service by visiting these institutions, not on specified days, but at unthought-of hours or seasons; for instance, get up a little earlier and go and insist on joining the children at their breakfast table. On other occasions, demand admission to the schoolroom, and observe the countenance and manner of those paid to instruct these children; in short, observe the deportment of the paid servants of the institution all the way through. A still better way, by-the-bye, of following your Saviour and serving your generation, would be to take some such children yourselves and bring them up with all the love and care with which you bring up your own, or would have done so had God granted you the privilege. It will be a happy day for England when Christian ladies transfer their sympathies from poodles and terriers to destitute and starving children!

Sixth. Another scheme, perhaps the lowest of these material systems of salvation, is the **feeding system**.

I mean that system in which large sums of money are spent, merely upon providing some special feast for those who are well known to be, as a rule, almost without food. Now, I think you will all believe me when I say that I rejoice in every bite or sup provided for the needy, but I cannot help seeing how monstrously all this exhibits the recklessness of the Christian world as to the greater needs of the perishing. Some of the most intelligent and highly placed people in the country may be seen looking complacently on upon the ragged, hungry crowd, who are eagerly devouring the only good meal perhaps which they have had for a twelvemonth, or which is likely to be within their reach for as long again, looking on without apparently having their sense of satisfaction in the slightest degree ruffled by the thought (if such people ever do think) about the lives which these "poor creatures" live during the other 364 days of the year! Such observers do not seem to look behind the staring eyes and hollow cheeks and savage ferocity of the eaters. The starving hunger, the devilish dispositions and abject despair of the "**man inside**" does not seem to trouble them.

Now, what I want to impress upon you is, not that these bodily wants are unworthy of the attention bestowed upon them,--for I regard it as a crying shame that such wants should not have a thousand times more attention, and in a thousand times more comprehensive fashion than they at present receive,--but what I complain of is, the attempt to substitute any or all of these for a thorough work in the heart; and when such "charity" is carried out on the long pole system, and yet paraded in the name of Christ, I regard it as rather an insult than a credit to His name. It seems to me that the Popular Christianity which would put these things in the place of the gospel is only another of the clever shams of the devil by which to ruin our race, and to turn aside God's people to broken cisterns, only insuring a more eternal weight of misery at the cost of a little present relief.

Oh, friends, you who have health, talent, and means, make up your own minds on which side you will act. Remember that in the light of that judgment which is coming on, it will appear worse than useless to have expended your energies and powers on doing that kind of good which will **NOT LAST**, which will, in fact, by itself, serve the enemies' purpose rather than otherwise. Either do as Christ commands you, or cease to call your work by His name. Do not let any one delude you with the idea that you are **following Christ**, or doing that work which is peculiarly His, in contradistinction to all merely human benevolence and earthly salvation, unless you are seeking **first** His kingdom, both within your own soul and every one else's.

The Second Scheme

The second of these schemes of salvation without a Saviour is even worse than that which I have already described; for while that tended to turn the thoughts of men from the world to come to some good or advantage of a temporal kind, this would lay a degrading hand upon eternity itself, and, under pretense of elevating humanity, would push it into a future life with its deepest intuitions all scorched up, and its highest aspirations disappointed and blighted.

Here, again, are to be found various sects, etc.

First comes **universalism**. This theory would make men into mere puppets, who for the time being are allowed to be the prey of an evil power, but after a certain amount of suffering are to be picked up by a better power. Like some unhappy country whose patriotic force has been crushed out of it until it has become the helpless prize, first of one monarch and then of another, so the kingdom of the human soul is to pass from evil to good and from Satan to God.

The blackest wretch on earth, who has made his home a hell, and spread moral ruin as widely as he could reach, is, according to this theory, to be saved even as the purest saint; for "all men" are to be saved--by repentance and a holy life, if they choose, if not, still they are to be saved--by their own free will, if they have fixed their affections on things above; but if, on the other hand, they have loved sin and vice, and committed all the catalogue of crimes, still salvation is to come out of devilry, and a clean thing out of an unclean! To try to make men believe in such a system seems to me to be no less insulting to their understandings than it is shocking to their consciences, and defiant of the plainest teachings of Scripture common sense and analogy.

The extent of our present knowledge with respect to a better world is that it is the abode of those "who have overcome" evil. Its songs are of victory! Its inhabitants renounced the mark of the beast on earth, washed their robes and made them white in the blood of the Lamb, kept the commandments of God, and through much tribulation were faithful unto death. To this assemblage of crowned victors, the universalist would introduce the man who, while on earth, overcame not evil but good, who was victorious, not over his own passions, the temptations of the devil, and the forces of evil around him, but over the dictates of his own conscience, the influences and agencies which God put in operation in order to save him, and over all the forces of righteousness with which he came in contact. Strange mercy! to send a man like this to a heaven where every song would remind him of defeat and degradation, and every crown and psalm make conspicuous his false and ignominious position. Strange justice also which gives the prize to him who never won it, nay, who despised the conditions of the contest, and refused to enter the lists!

Second in this scheme comes what I shall designate as the **all love theory**.

The propounders of this theory, without daring actually to contest the great facts of revelation, would have us be silent about the most serious of them, lest we should shock the people. They tell us gravely that men will be "repelled from the gospel," if its truths about judgment and hell are not kept in the background; tell, say they, about the Father's love, but do not talk about "damnation" and "the wrath to come." Strange mercy this, to let men perish rather than tell them that sin breeds a hell from which none can deliver them. What should we think of a father too merciful to tell us the truth? Should we not say he was cruel? The child playing on your hearth-rug might well complain if you will not tell him that fire burns, because, forsooth, he might think you cruel to have it there, and so you leave him to find it out by falling in! "Hush, do not frighten the people;" sing to them, talk sweetly to them; there are no modern words for hell and such-like horrors. In ancient days there were prophets, whose fiery warnings of judgment to come led whole nations to repentance, but men think they know better now. The God who sent those poor old fanatics to speak plain words of wrath and denunciation is not their God. His words of burning reproof and fearful threatening is not **their** burden. Their message is some "sweet text" tied to a bunch of flowers; their burden can be given by "Saturday evenings for the people," where "comic readings," "gymnastics," "secular music by the choir" are the converting measures deemed most suitable. Alas! alas! such maudlin souls are not worthy to deal with the things of eternity! Who wants in the hospital a man too 'tender" to probe the wound, too "merciful" to amputate the mortifying limb, too "loving" to say with firmness, Do this, bear this, or die? Away with such a sentimental surgeon, you would cry; send him to pick rose leaves, where his feeble hands will do no mischief. And yet these over-merciful friends I am talking about would spiritually elevate the masses by twaddling to them in their sins and rebellion, about love, sweetness, and peace, when, if they did not shut their ears, and were willing to catch the sound, they would hear the thundering echoes from every sinner's conscience, "There is no peace to the wicked;" "Wrath to come, wrath to come!"

Third. Next in this catalogue of modern salvations comes the **theory of doubt.**

These doubters, while manifestly very shaky as to their own theory, argue that all is "too uncertain for us to speak positively as to eternity." As we have before noted, their scheme for elevating men is to teach know-nothingness. They seen to think that doubt in itself is something very ennobling, that it, in things spiritual, for in things temporal they have faith enough, and also exact it from others. They claim explicit trust in their business relations, perfect confidence in their domestic lives, but appear to think that to doubt the **great God** and His revelation will somehow prove a great blessing and benefit to mankind; "as to eternal things it is not seemly to speak positively."

In yonder back street, ah, even in the worst dens of vice, are found men who have in the depths of their sinful hearts some hidden memory, which is the link to holy things. Perhaps they have stood when boys by the dying bed of some humble believing father, who declared in his last hours that **he knew** in whom he had believed; or perhaps, even in the later and blacker days of their lives, they have seen a little one go from their own dark homes with a heavenly smile upon its face, and the words, "Jesus has come to fetch me," on its lips; and these men believe without a doubt in the God who, somehow, made their fathers and their children know Him, and some day they mean to turn to Him; but the chains of an evil life are holding them down with the "masses" of desperate and dangerous sinners around them. To these the modern scheme comes with its new light, and lays its withering touch on these memories of good. "We cannot know," it says; "women may have dreamt, and children believed, old men may have had their sick fancies, but it is better to be without that which is delusive; the only thing is that all is uncertain, the manly thing is to doubt."

Ah! rich man, you may sit in your palace-like home, where nothing unpleasant is now allowed to enter, and it may seem little loss to you, so far, that our belief in eternal things has been loosened; but to the poor man in his bare life, and to the man who is bound by some sinful chain of vice, and whose earthly career has not another gleam of hope, it becomes the final stroke of misery and degradation to make him think that he cannot know with any certainty any better things than those which now surround him. If there is not anywhere in the universe a Saviour's hand, whose clasp he may yet feel, and on whose strength he may depend to draw him up out of his drunken jail-bird existence to something purer and better, some day, when he shall have made up his mind to be saved, then his one door of hope is closed, and he realizes, with a bitterness which will drown itself in fresh outbursts of sin and villainy, that there **is no** true light or guide anywhere for anybody. Granted that the one guide is untrustworthy, the one beacon-light possibly false, he is out on the sea of life without a spark of hope or cheer. Shipwreck and eternal ruin may be the next event at any hour.

Fourth. **"The Christian free-thinkers"** next claim our attention.

These are bolder than the latter class, denying whatever seems to them to be objectionable in the Scriptures. The inspiration of the Bible is to them on a level with that of Shakespeare or Homer, and for anything they do not like they have a free rendering, or a cool excision. They would take away what they fancy to be stumbling-blocks in the path of men, without stopping to consider whether God Himself placed them there as guiding-posts. Ah, what contempt such men would feel for the word "free," if it were applied in other ways. Who would tolerate the "free" soldier, who set up his own notions as to military matters, and at the critical hour of the fight was found obeying and leading others to obey orders which had been altered by the omission of all which he considered objectionable! Who would for long be retained in her Majesty's household who should presume to alter the rules of court behaviour, and to expunge what he deemed irksome? And yet the revelation which is to train servants for the eternal household of the King of kings, and the laws laid down by the Lord of hosts, by which His battles are to be fought, may be treated with a free hand, and tinkered and paired--obeyed or disobeyed--according to the notions of men who love their own will better than anything else in heaven or on earth! Alas, I fear it may be said of these doubters that "while they promise men liberty, they themselves are servants to corruption," and I would remind them "how that the Lord, having saved the people out of the land of Egypt, afterwards destroyed them that **believed not**."

We might go on to multiply these modern schemes for the improvement and elevation of man, for they are legion, and some of them doubtless propounded by those who have much real concern and compassion for the multitudes, but which all the more, because there is so much of good in them, are the most dangerous and ruinous to the highest interests of mankind.

Take away from the way-faring man the absolute certainty which he feels about the truth of the gospel, and where do you leave him? Wretched and hopeless in the very centre of his being. You may have fed his body, you may have clothed and housed him, you may have educated his children, you may have nursed him in sickness and comforted him in sorrow; but for all this he is left on the moors to wander and die in desolation and darkness, in spite of all your feeding and all your loving rush-lights.

This sort of compassion is the most cruel *ignis fatuus* the devil ever invented. Depend upon it, you cannot be more merciful than Jesus, who says to-day to you and to all men, "He that believeth shall be saved, and he that believeth not shall be damned."

The Dying Love of Christ

We propose now to consider in juxtaposition with all these modern schemes for the elevation of mankind, on which we have been remarking, **that** one which is universally admitted to be the model scheme; the ideal of all that is lovely, tender, ennobling, and comprehensive.

The scheme of Christ, with its aims and modes, as shown in the story of His life-compassion for the world. I contend that the compassion of Jesus stands out distinguished as of another kind from all the philanthropic plans which we have been considering.

First: By its **clear perception of the worst feature of man's condition**.

No doubt the Saviour's heart ached in sympathy with the mass of human sorrow, sickness, and poverty brought before Him. Where we have only a glimpse of men's trouble as we move hurriedly up and down among them, He has the whole sad story unfolded to Him, and His keen love responded tenderly to every cry for help. Nevertheless, He was never diverted from the **great central danger**. To Him the sorrowful troubled crowd were not merely poor and suffering, not merely oppressed by unjust laws, and crowded into badly constructed dwellings,--not merely hungry, hard-worked, and comfortless; these were incidents which He sometimes alleviated and more often shared, but the crowning peril, the absolutely certain woe which eclipsed, in His sight, every other, was the **loss of the soul**. He flings aside contemptuously the thought that living well in this world was a real benefit. The fool of all the world, the man who in His opinion stood most awful risk, is drawn by Him in a parable sketch which is little dwelt on in these days. This fool in Christ's picture was the rich man with bursting barns and "so much goods" that he knew not how to dispose of them. He was a man who had been elevated by education enough, at any rate, to enable him to do a good business; he enjoyed the benefits of a good dwelling, good food, and, doubtless, the best society within his reach; and yet he was a fool, and Christ holds him up as the last sample of such, simply because he left his soul in jeopardy.

Again, Christ draws another picture, blacker and more awful yet, and again He selects the rich man (the very man, remember, who had enjoyed the best of this worlds benefits and who also was kind to the poor Lazarus), and yet Christ draws aside the veil of the future world, and shows where earthly elevation landed him.

"The rich man died, and was buried; and in hell he lift up his eyes, being in torments, and seeth Abraham afar off, and Lazarus in his bosom. And he cried and said, Father Abraham, have mercy on me, and send Lazarus, that he may dip the tip of this finger in water, and cool my tongue; for I am tormented in this flame. But Abraham said,

~ Popular Christianity ~

Son, remember that thou in thy lifetime receivedst thy good things, and likewise Lazarus evil things: but now he is comforted, and thou art tormented. And beside all this, between us and you there is a great gulf fixed: so that they which would pass from thence to you cannot; neither can they pass to us, that would come from thence."

What! could it be Christ who talked about a man in fire, a man crying for a drop of water, and denied even this small boon! Could it be Christ who talked about torment, and showed this vision of despair; the tender, loving, merciful Christ! Ah, He showed it, because **HE SAW IT**; because this was the real danger, from which He had come to deliver! Because He knew that the sick beggar, covered with undressed wounds, and with scarce an alleviating circumstance to assuage his sufferings, might have the eternal compensation which should make his earthly troubles seem like a dream, if only his soul was right, if only he was "rich towards God." Christ showed this, because it was the one thing which no one else saw. The human needs of men were apparent enough to many benevolent people in His day, including the rich giver who was going to hell, but the crying soul needs, which had brought him out of heaven, the hopeless woe to which even the rich and happy were drifting--the undying worm, the quenchless fire, were the visions of sorrow which He only saw, and which His tenderest compassion betrayed itself in seeking to relieve. "For what shall it profit a man, if he shall gain the whole world and lose his own soul?" may be taken as indicating the foundation principle of His entire scheme of redemption.

Second: Christ's compassion is distinguished from all other compassions by its **plain, cutting, personal dealing**.

"He would eat with sinners," talk familiarly and tenderly with the worst on earth, and lay His hands upon the most loathsome, but He was incapable of dealing lightly with their sin.

Imagine Christ giving an entertainment, and spending the evening in frivolous talk, in order that He might humour sinners and attract them to Himself! Imagine Him allowing His little band of disciples to sing current songs and read "amusing selections" for a couple of hours at a time to keep people out of worse company! No, He was too tenderly compassionate for souls, who He knew might end their time on earth at any moment, thus to fool away His chance. He never lost an opportunity of talking straight to them about their sins, the interests of their souls, and the claims of His Father's law. The young ruler comes to Him, and he is so lovable, so moral, so food, might he not have been allowed to join the little band of disciples, and to have gained light gradually? "Yet lackest thou one thing" was pronounced all the more clearly because "He loved him." "Sell that thou hast, and follow Me" rang out all the more distinctly because He could offer treasure for the **soul**.

The compassion of Jesus was not of the maudlin kind which leaves men their "little indulgences," and shrinks from being "too hard" on them, where hardness is the indispensable condition of salvation. "If thy right hand offend thee, cut it off; if they right eye offend thee, pluck it out," He mercilessly prescribes; better, He decides, be maimed and suffering here, than be cast into "eternal fire."

As to the religious ideas of His day, He walked straight across them with a cutting "Woe unto you!" Woe! woe! was the one cry with which He met the teachers and professors of His time, provoking their bitterest hate and animosity. "Making clean the outside platter, while within are dead men's bones," was His short description of them and their doings. He upset the nice little fashions which had sprung up around the temple worship with a whip of cords. "Publicans and harlots shall enter the kingdom before you," He told the grand professors who listened to Him. He inflicted the faithful wounds of a friend, in order that He might awaken them to their danger and lead them to seek the only remedy.

Third: Christ's compassion was in direct contrast with all mere human benevolence in its "**other worldliness**."

No one will dispute that He possessed the power to elevate the masses in a temporal sense, by bestowing on them all those benefits at which modern philanthropy aims. He could have fed them by a miracle every day, as easily as on the two occasions when He multiplied the bread; and who could have lectured on science, or history, or invention, so clearly, so perfectly, as He to whom all knowledge must be an open book? He could have brought into His services those twelve legions of angels, and taken an earthly kingdom, from which He could have dispensed wealth and prosperity to all around; but He indicated **His** scheme for elevating and saving the people when He said "I am the Way"--to another sphere, another realm, not of earthly good, but of heavenly. When He was asked for the posts of honour in His kingdom, He made it clear that He was leading to another and higher world through a "baptism" and with a "cup" of suffering and poverty in this.

Fourth: Christ's compassion stands out in its **spiritual fellowship**.

The King of kings makes eternal friends of the fishermen. "He did not visit the poor," "He did not elevate their sad lot," and walk on His own high path, having His fellowship, His joys, His sorrows apart from them; but He shared His life with them in a holy comradeship. He did not live in the style and companionship of the worldly Pharisee, and occasionally visit Peter, James, and John, and hold meetings for the working classes; no, He lived with them and became education, elevation, salvation, and all to them by His blessed fellowship. "Ye are my friends," said He, and "all things that I have heard of My Father, I have made known unto you." His heart had no reserves from these men. John's head could lean on His breast, and Mary could sit at His feet, with the consciousness that they were taken into His confidence, and were indeed as brethren.

That they could not always understand Him was their fault, not His; but their slowness and dulness never wearied His compassion, not caused Him to seek friends elsewhere. He called His three fishermen to Him when He was about to put forth any wonderful exercise of power. He wanted Peter, James, and John, when He was raising the dead, and took them to share His joy on the mount of transfiguration. He craved for their presence in His last agony, and desired no better provision for His mother, when He hung upon the cross, that the home that one of them could afford.

Fifth: The compassion of Jesus is yet further distinguished by its **Divine faith, and hope, and action**.

He had faith in the possibilities of these people, which possibilities would not have been very apparent to any other eye. He believed in the transforming power of the Spirit which He could send them. His hope was not chilled by stupidity, or foolishness, or non-comprehension on the part of disciples or outsiders. Mighty compassion must that have been that could live thirty years on such terms with such men, and never falter or turn back. Many a fine scheme of modern benevolence dies and goes out when the people who are to be benefited get to be known! "Such wretches," "so ungrateful," "so presuming," "so hopeless." But Christ hoped all things, believed all things, until the Peter who was afraid of a servant girl stood triumphant before the three thousand converts. Christ kept

His little band together, although He knew there was a traitor amongst them,--the traitor who would betray Him, and sell Him for money into the hands of His enemies. Christ forbore and worked with John until the man who wanted fire from heaven to burn up sinners became an apostle of love. Christ made the Samaritan harlot woman into His ambassador on the spot; Christ made sound men of the lepers, and sane divines of the mad. He called the devils out of those whom they tormented, and then let loose the whole strange flock of ex-harlots, maniacs, and lepers, to tell His praises and to gather others to His presence. Christ went up to Calvary undismayed by His perfect knowledge of sinful, perverse, opposing men, to die for the whole ungrateful race. Christ hoped and believed in His own blackest hour for the dying blackguard at His side, and saved him as he hung there. Talk about "eternal hope!" Is not this the eternal hope which saves to the uttermost now and here?

Sixth: The compassion of Jesus is further distinguished by His ever **going straight to the one end**.

The whole work of Christ was aimed at the salvation of men's **souls**. And this is not the less true because He also benefited their bodies by healing their diseases and sympathising with their sorrows.

This latter side of His work is much dwelt upon in these days, and yet it was a merely incidental part. If He had come to remove earthly suffering, poverty, oppression, and distress, He would, as I have pointed out, certainly have gone about it in a different way. He would have aimed at riches and position and ease, in order that He might have shared them with His own chosen ones. He would have sought to build up an earthly kingdom, where men should neither hunger nor thirst, nor be sick, nor die; and it would have been a far easier task than the founding of that new invisible kingdom which we have already tried to describe, where only the spiritual and eternal should be of much importance. In comparison, how much easier to have drawn crowds if He had always given them their dinner, than to hold followers who should enter into the mysterious doctrine, "I am the Bread of life;" "ye must be born again!"

But He did feed the multitudes, and He did heal the sick! Yes, but He gave up the former when He found that they followed Him for that only, and His acts of healing were flashes of the Divine power within Him, rather than the "work given Him to do." "I came to call sinners to repentance," "I am come to set the daughter-in-law against her mother-

~ Popular Christianity ~

in-law, and a man's foes shall be they of his own household." "I came to bring fire on earth." "I came not to send peace, but a sword." These sayings, and multitudes of others, were descriptive of a **spiritual** mission, and yet He was most tender, as we readily trace, to every suffering, needy creature who came in contact with Him. His pity was boundless for the lame, the blind, and the deaf, and His loving heart must have grieved over much in the sea of human misery brought before Him, of which we never hear. The truest love must ever seek the highest good of its object, sometimes even with forgetfulness of important lesser advantages. He gave the great rule by which **His** compassion for men's necessities was guided, when He said, "Seek first the kingdom of God, and His righteousness; and all other things shall be added unto you."

Seventh: The compassion of Jesus stands out in contrast with all other in **its devotion unto death**.

He was too merciful to men to spare them the bitter truths of hell, or conceal from them the punishments due to transgression; but on Himself He had no compassion.

If the penalty was indeed so awful, He would share it. He too would bear the curse, the shame, the agony of dying for sin, so far as could for the sinless One be possible.

How brightly this compassion shines out against that of many who profess so much for the suffering and the lost. Watch the people who talk the most loudly of their tenderness, and will not say one word of the "outer darkness" and the hell fire of which He said so much. Where are their Calvarys? Are they remarkable for cross bearing? Are they noted for self-denial, or is it in word only, and not in deed, that they are more compassionate than Jesus? They do not like to repeat to the poor His terrible words of warning. May it not be because they are unwilling to **act** toward the poor as He did?

No rough living, no fishermen friends, no hungry, weary days, no homeless nights, no persecution and contempt--above all, no scourge, no crown of thorns, no march up to Golgotha, no nailing to the cross, no agony, no dying for the salvation of men! There can be no other dying love than that which causes the real dying. Do settle that in your minds, for without a dying, a real, complete, and eternal separation between your old self and the new self, which means to live and die for others, you cannot be a true disciple of Jesus Christ, or an eternal benefactor to your race. You may not come to any such terrible end as your Master did, for as a rule in outward things the servant is above his Lord, but in some way or another you are doubtless called to follow Him in a path full of suffering and self-denial, in a road of shame in which you will find yourself completely cut off, alas, from the rest of mankind; but without this daily dying, this true following of Him, do not expect to be able to do any lasting good to those who are perishing around you.

Let no benevolent projects, no magnificent phrases deceive you. The good done to mankind by the poor fisherman who spoke the truth, the whole truth, and nothing but the truth, has surpassed all the achievements of modern philanthropy as far as the noon-day sun surpasses the rushlight.

If you want to elevate the masses, go and ask **HIM** how to do it, and if the answer comes, "Take up thy cross and follow Me," **OBEY**.

LECTURE IV

POPULAR CHRISTIANITY: ITS COWARDLY SERVICE *v.* THE REAL WARFARE

The subject for this afternoon is The Cowardly Service of Popular Christianity in contrast with the Real Warfare which Christ demands of His People.

I should like to say before I commence, that I hope, nay, I believe, that many of my audience will give me credit for speaking the truth in love; that although some things I may have to say may sound cutting, and will be cutting, as all truth when it comes in contact with error must be--it would cease to be truth if it were not--yet that I do not speak these things censoriously. If I know anything of my own heart and experience, I can say I do not speak these things harshly, but painfully and reluctantly. But they have been burnt into my soul during twenty-one years of public work, by absolute personal contact with the evils of which I speak. I have forborne long, hoping that some one more able would take up this sword, until I sometimes fear that I have been guilty of withholding my sword from blood--God knows not for my own sake, for since I came to the crucifixion of myself I have not cared much what men might say of me; but I have forborne sometimes under a mistaken notion of dealing gently with, and of hiding, the sins of professed Christians for fear of
hurting the kingdom. But some three or four years ago the Lord took me to task, more especially on this matter, and showed me that I had no more right to palliate a wrong state of things in His professing people than in open sinners--that we ought to examine **ourselves**, judge **ourselves**, and reprove **ourselves** and each other, so that we might redeem His name from the awful effects of our inconsistency, and of our coming so far short of the standard which Christ has set up for us. Therefore what I saw this afternoon, and in my following lectures, please to bear in mind I only say because I **MUST**, and because I could not die in peace if I had not said it. That I shall be criticised and condemned I fully expect, and that in exact proportion to the force with which the truths shall be demonstrated in every man's conscience. But be assured that this effort has cost me many a tear and

prayer, and much thought and self-abandonment. I think I can say to those persons here who may be cut the most severely, and to those who are not here to whom my words refer, I could gladly go down at their feet and wash them with my tears, if I could thus bring about a better state of things.

I want to remark first, that Jesus Christ came to establish the **kingdom of God upon earth**; that He intended this kingdom to be a literal kingdom, that is, as truly a kingdom as any of the kingdoms of this world; that He intended it to be a holy kingdom, a kingdom of righteousness, and consequently separate from, and above, all other kingdoms; that Christ continually spoke of His followers as a community, existing in the midst of another kingdom or community, having its own laws and principles and aims
entirely distinct and separate from the world. He not only made it separate, but He ordained that it should be kept separate, and He did not fail to give the most emphatic cautions and prohibitions against any amalgamation whatever between the forces of His kingdom and the forces of the kingdom of Satan, in the midst of which His kingdom was established.

Further, He put forth the claim, as the King and Sovereign of this kingdom, to the highest affection, allegiance, and homage of the hearts of His subjects, representing Himself as a King in a sense entirely beyond and above all earthly sovereigns. He represented Himself as reigning, not by virtue of outward power, but by virtue of the inward love, devotion, and adoration of His subjects; and thus more perfectly and completely over their outward lives than any earthly king could pretend to do.

Further, the avowed purpose of Jesus Christ was to propagate and extend this kingdom over the whole earth.

In this respect only was He the originator of a new dispensation, for God had already a kingdom in the earth, although it was of a national and sectarian character. Jesus Christ came to break down the walls of partition between Jew and Gentile, and to let out, so to speak, the mercy, goodness, and grace of God to the whole race. Henceforth there was to be "neither Greek nor Jew, ... barbarian, Scythian, bond not free; but Christ is all, and in all."

But as in Adam all had died, so in Christ should all he made alive; as all men had lost their souls in Adam, so all should have the opportunity, subject to that free choice without which either salvation

~ Popular Christianity ~

or damnation would be a mere figure of speech, and without which a man would be no more capable of salvation than an ox,--subject only to such a choice, every son and daughter of Adam should have the provision in Christ of eternal salvation.

Then, further, Jesus Christ ordained and arranged that this kingdom of His should be propagated in the world by human instrumentality. Why, we do not know. There might be many reasons, but the main one probably was that the human being, himself transformed, restored to God and to His image, and inspired with His love, would be the most **effectual** ambassador that God could send.

Another reason might be that Christ chose to put this honour on His own brethren after the Spirit--those whom He has redeemed from amongst men, and who have chosen Him as their Sovereign, with His cross and its consequences, in preference to the pleasures, riches, or honours of this world.

Or, third, it might be that no other instrumentality would be so calculated to bring glory to His Father, the weakness of the human agent exhibiting most perfectly the excellency of the Divine power.

Note further, that the establishment of this kingdom over all the earth means, of course, resistance and opposition from those nations already in possession.

And here is a wonderful analogy between the establishment of the kingdom of Christ and the subjugation of Canaan to the Israelites. God had promised that land to Abraham long years before, and spoke of it as already belonging to his descendants; nevertheless they had to go and conquer it in His strength. So God has given the kingdom of this earth to His Son. In the end the kingdoms of this world are to become the kingdoms of our God and of His Christ; but we have to go and conquer them, just as the Israelites had to conquer Canaan, in the faith, and by the strength, of our God. It has only been for want of faith that the world has not been conquered long ago. Oh, what a delusion many Christians labour under with respect to the extension of the kingdom of God! They have a notion that the kingdom is to take the world by stealth; that men are to be turned to God without any connection of means with the event; that it is going to be done by a sort of internal miracle, and the Church has been waiting for this miracle for 1800 years. Consequently the work is not **done**, because this notion is in direct opposition to the orders and ordination of the King. If ever the world is subdued, it will be by His servants carrying out their Lord's instructions, and setting themselves to subdue it. It will be by bringing all the wisdom, skill, and force of their humanity, allied with divinity, as the early disciples did, and turning that force upon the rebel world. It will be done by **hard, desperate fighting**, if the great fundamental principles laid down in this Bible are to be relied on, and in no other way, because the nations in possession will never let you subdue them and take them for God without opposition. Christ systematically foretold and depicted this opposition, and gave His disciples to understand that they would have to wage **WAR** with all the power of those who were possessed of evil, and who were profiting by evil, and that it would be no easy conquest.

He told them they would have to go and subdue this evil by good, this unrighteousness by righteousness. The spirit of the devil would have to be driven out of man by the power of the Spirit of God dwelling in **them**. This He taught as plainly and persistently as He taught anything. If we wanted an illustration of the continuance of this spirit of opposition in the earth, we might find it in the events that have lately transpired in Switzerland. A little force of godly people, without any of the peculiarities about which there had been such a hue and cry in England, without an instrument of music, without a banner or flag, or procession, or open-air service, without even a uniform, had only to commence to live Jesus Christ over again, and to carry out His orders in thrusting His claims on their fellow-men, when wicked rulers combined with those who profit by the vilest kinds of vice to mob them, drive them out, put them down, or kill them, as the case might be. Why? Because the instinct of the evil one recognised the Spirit of Jesus Christ. The devil always knows where the Spirit of Jesus Christ is, and he knows something else; he knows where it is **not**, and where it is not he lets well alone!

"Oh!" people say, "the world is different in these days from what it was in the days of Jesus Christ and Paul." Is it? Try it on the **same lines**, and you will soon find out how far different it is. The very essence of the spirit of evil is antagonistic to the spirit of good. Good and evil are as diametrically opposed to each other as ever; therefore they can never be brought into contact without conflict, without war, and sometimes of the most deadly kind, ending in the death and martyrdom of the saints. I was amused with the exemplification of this some weeks ago. As one of our female officers was walking up Clapton, a band of lads were hooting after her, "Hallelujah!" "Jesus

~ Popular Christianity ~

Christ!" "Salvation!" and other beautiful names; for in whatever voice they be hissed out, they cannot make such words ugly. They were hissing these names after her as she walked meekly and quietly along. At length she turned suddenly to them and said, "What are you doing this for? I have never done you any harm. I am walking peaceably along the road; why are you shouting after me?" They were all so taken aback that they stood breathless for a moment, then one of them, I suppose a little bolder than the rest, and at least an honest lad, said, "It is because you are good and we are bad." Ah! that was the truth for once. That was the expression, in his rough way, of the eternal principle, that there must be conflict between good and evil; and the greater good you bring in conflict with evil, the more the evil will range and try for the mastery. Hence, the world treated Him who was the very personification of the Father's holiness, worse than it ever treated any other human being, because He was the concentration of goodness, and therefore the devil did his worst on Him; and just as we approximate to His character will the devil do his worst on us.

Further, Christ taught His soldiers to expect the opposition of devils.

I suppose most of you believe in evil spirits who have access to the human mind. I wish, if you do not, you could have some of the experience of the Salvation Army; I think you would then. If there are evil spirits, if they have access to this world, and if they are interested in circumventing the plans of God, it only stands to sense that they should influence their servants to fight in opposition to the servants of God. This opposition was foretold by Christ, and His servants were warned against it, and provided for it. He said to His apostles when He commissioned them, "Behold, I send you forth as sheep among wolves, but lo, I am with you always." And again to Paul, I will be with thee, "delivering thee from the people, and from the Gentiles, unto whom now I send thee." Why? Because He knew the opposition which their mission would provoke. He said, "Think not that I am come to send peace on earth: I came not to send peace, but a sword." Wherever the true Christ appears, there must the sword come to the dividing asunder of everything evil, and there must also come the sword of provocation. Even the nearest and dearest relatives rise up to persecute those who truly follow the Christ. This must continue to be so while good and evil continue in contact, and the fact that modern Christianity has ceased, as a rule, to provoke opposition, is one of the deadliest signs of its effeteness. As a rule, the world and modern Christianity go comfortably on together. They are so actuated by one common pathway, that you see very little collision between them. The world alone has very little to complain of, and so it lets them alone. May God help, and quickly mend or end it.

    Further, I want you to note, that, notwithstanding all the danger involved in this deadly warfare, which Jesus Christ represented it to be,--for He did not deceive them, but told them plainly that all men would hate them, that they would probably have to follow Him to martyrdom and death,--nevertheless, they accepted the mission. I grant that they were a little time in coming to comprehend it; I grant that it took some time to free them from their national and sectarian prejudices. Peter had to receive his lesson through the visions of the sheet let down from heaven, before he understood the true genus of his mission. But when he and the other apostles did comprehend it,--and that was the difference between them and modern apostles,--when they saw the work to which the Master called them, they joyfully embraced it. They did not stop to confer with flesh and blood, or to reason what it would cost them, to ask about salaries, or houses, or friends; they embraced the mission and went, and carried it out with their lives in their hands; and oh, how magnificently they succeeded! What a large portion of the world they subdued in comparison with their numbers and facilities, for, remember, there were no railways in those days to speed them from town to town, and city to city; there were no telegraphs to fly before them with their announcements; no printing presses to herald their coming with posters and handbills and all manner of notices: they had none of the facilities which we possess in these days for quickening their speed, or how gladly would they have availed themselves of them! What gigantic success they attained, because they carried out their mission on the lines which Jesus Christ had laid down. Is it not true that just in proportion as their successors have followed in their steps, they have been successful in propagating the gospel? We all know that the stars in the heavenly firmament, the men and women whose names stand out with extra brilliancy on the page of history, as having been successful in pushing this glorious warfare, have been the men and women who took their lives in their hands, and followed their Master without respect to consequences; who came out straight and **clear from the world** and set themselves to do their work, irrespective of what men might say or do to them. And

~ Popular Christianity ~

we know what mighty conquests some of them achieved, and therefore we may reason that if all Christ's professed disciples had followed in the same track, a million times greater results would have been attained.

Let me put a practical question here. How many are there here who have comprehended the task? How many are there to whom the Spirit of God has said in unmistakable language, "Come out from amongst the ungodly or the half-hearted, and be separate, and I will touch your lips with a live coal from off My altar, and will make you fishers of men"? Did you embrace the mission? Have you gone forth following your Master, carrying His cross and seeking the souls of men? If not, what will you say to Him in the great day of account?

Further, in looking at the requirements of the King, and at the history of the early apostles and disciples, I charge it on modern Christianity, that its professors do not even **comprehend the first principles of this warfare**, much less do they set themselves to carry it on to the ends of the earth.

The service rendered to the King and to the kingdom in these days is, alas, with very few exceptions, of a very milk-and-watery type, of a very short-weight character, and the great effort of the majority of its teachers, judging from their writings, and from what we see and know of their public services and of their private lives, seems to be intended to make things comfortable all around. "Peace, peace," is the continual cry, when there is no peace. As one of the bishops said a little while ago, "We hear a great deal about Church defence; we ought to be hearing about Church aggression." Yes, alas! in the great mass if instances when these modern Christians do fight, it is over opinions and ceremonies with their own children, inside their own walls, instead of with the enemy outside. They are far more valiant in defending some ceremonial of the Church, than they are in defending the cross of Christ in the presence of its adversaries. They are far more concerned in propagating their "ism" than the kingdom of righteousness, peace, and joy in the Holy Ghost. Alas, that it should be so; but such is the fact, and it is patent to every enlightened observer.

Jesus Christ did not call us to fight each other, but He called us to present one bold front to the enemy. He bade us go and take captive the hearts and souls of men, and not merely to change their **opinions**. Get a man's heart right, and his opinions will soon follow. But you may be tinkering at his intellect till the hour of his death, and he will not be a whit nearer heaven, but perchance nearer hell, than if he had been let alone.

Further, these modern Christians, as a rule, do not see any **NEED for the fight**.

They hide themselves under some vain, false notions of the sovereignty of God. Oh, how often they have made my heart ache when I have been trying to arouse them to do something for the kingdom. They say, "God is a sovereign, and He will accomplish His purposes out of all this sin and ruin;" and so they sit comfortably down and let things drift; and they have drifted to some purpose, have they not? In this so-called Christian country, in this nineteenth century, they have drifted to about as near perdition as they well could, without absolutely bringing hell on the earth. They have drifted socially as well as spiritually. Look at the state of the nation. Look at the godlessness, the injustice, the falseness, the blasphemy, the uncleanness and the debauchery everywhere! Do you ever look at the condition of things close to your doors and your churches? the worse than heathen beastliness into which thousands of our neglected neighbors, rich and poor alike, have sunk? If only half the professing Christians of London had followed in their Master's steps for one twelve months, such things would have been impossible, utterly impossible!

I repeat, Jesus Christ has ordained and provided that His people are to set themselves to stem these torrents of moral and social pollution; they are to go and beard the lion in his den; to face the slaves of sin, open their eyes, and bring them down to His feet, just as much as were His early followers; and never till we do it shall we realize a better state of things. All the legislation, education, or provision of better dwellings, as I shall hereafter try to demonstrate, won't touch the moral cancer, the spring of all this wickedness and misery; nothing will do it until the Christians rise up to do their Master's bidding. But I say, they do not see any need for it, and they try to quiet us who do. You have to prove, and argue, and drive, and almost show them damnation before you can get a bit of service of any sort of them. They have no **heart** for the fight. They do not **feel** these things. As God said of the fallen and false prophets of the Jews, "They lay not these things to their hearts." They lay their own business to their hearts. You see it depicted on the countenances of these Christian men if the balance is on the wrong side; if bankruptcy stares them in the face, you soon find that out. These Christian women lay the

~ Popular Christianity ~

welfare of their own families or their hearts; you soon find out when a child is sick, or in any kind of disgrace or danger. But these same men and women can walk about the walls and see the desolations of Zion without any of these marks of distress or apprehension, without any such tears or groans.

They will manifest more anger against the people who urge them to fight, than they will against the enemy. A great many of them hate the Salvation Army for this more than for any other thing. They say "You are always at us: let us alone, we want peace." They want to be quiet and comfortable, and to have their religion in a snug, back-parlour fashion. Fight! they hate the name of fighting. Going out to face a mob! oh dear no, that is out of all question. How could you ever think of such a thing. Being mocked, and spit upon, and kicked, and buffetted, and perchance killed for Christ! they would think you were clean gone made. Some of these modern Christians have tried to put two or three of our people into asylums for nothing else. The moment anybody attempts really to obey Jesus Christ, they cry, "Mad! mad! away with such a fellow; he is not fit to live." What a veritable laughing-stock to hell such professed Christians make themselves. The devil says, "All right; let them alone. Let them go to their sanctuaries, let them have their creeds and ceremonies, let them sing their sweet hymns, and amuse themselves with their religious entertainments and their Bible classes; do not disturb them whatever you do, they are amongst my best and most successful allies." Oh, may God show us these things, and help us to set work to awaken every backslidden, lazy professor within reach of us.

Many of these latter day Christians are most zealous in building the sepulchres of the prophets, that is, of the saints--the spiritual warriors of bygone times. They are often great at lectures on these ancient worthies--Luther, George Fox, Wesley, and others, and they will listen most interestedly to a dissertation on their heroism, just as they would listen to a lecture on Shakespeare or Milton; but as to **imitating** their deeds of valour, it never enters their minds any more than if they had been inhabitants of another sphere. They simply go, in the great mass of instances, to have their intellects amused, their feelings tickled. It never dawns on them that **they** are to go and imitate the example of these heroes. They do not perceive that it ought equally to be the absorbing interest of **their own** lives, and that they are equally called to brave men and devils in propagating the kingdom of

61

Christ in the earth. They go home and live the coming week exactly as they lived the week that preceded it. They admire the men who laid down their lives for the King a hundred or three hundred years ago, and will perhaps put up a monument to their memory, but as to doing so themselves, or allowing themselves to come into the same circumstances of persecution, they would soon almost go to hell. I speak the things I know and have witnessed till my heart is sick.

Further, I charge it on popular Christianity that its professors are **ashamed of their colours** in the presence of the enemy.

They shrink from any open, straightforward confession of Christ before men. I maintain that it is not confessing Him to go to church or chapel once a week amongst those who go the same way with you. They do not confess Him on the exchange, in the bank, or in the streets of the city. Where do you see any one, or only on in a million, who comes out with any thorough-going, straightforward confession of Christ before the world? Where? There are a few Roman Catholic or high Church monastics, and whatever I may think of their errors and their mummeries, I always feel a measure of reverence when I pass them. I feel there is a man or woman who is willing to acknowledge his God before men, and who is not ashamed to come out and condemn the world, by being separate from it, and entering a protest against its fashions and its follies.

How many professing Christians are there of this day who go through the city of London in any attire, or with any kind of badge, that said to men and women, "I am a saint and a soldier of Jesus Christ"? And yet the soldiers of the queen are proud to do this in an enemy's country! I repeat, who is there that dare do it for Christ, except we fanatics of the Salvation Army?

I understand that a popular minister said the other day, speaking of the Salvation Army, that we were "playing at soldiers!" I will engage to say that if that minister will come with us for a single day, we will give him such a dose of fighting as he never had in his life before. We will send him home at night quite convinced that it is no playing at soldiers on our part. If he does not get his head broken, we will guarantee that his coat will be torn, or covered with mud or ochre, or something worse!

Playing at soldiers indeed! Let him doff his kid gloves, his gentleman's attire, and lay aside his **cigar**, and come with our lasses into the public-houses with the *War Cry* or a *Bible* under his arm, or

~ Popular Christianity ~

anything else that tells the inmates what he has come for, and he will find out whether we are playing at soldiers or not! I would like to put that man alongside one of our dear little female captains in a certain jail just now, and see whether such an experience, even for twenty-four hours, would not change his opinion. Such cruel stabs from professed Christian ministers are worse than the cruel mockings and scourgings of the enemy. "May the Lord not lay this sin to their charge." But to return to this shame-facedness in the Master's cause: it is time we had done with it; it is time we proclaimed ourselves; for we speak to numbers by our appearance to whom we can never speak by our words, and unless we confess Christ in our appearance in such instances, we cannot confess Him at all. Besides, why should we be ashamed of it? Why? The other day when I was driving though a low thoroughfare of London, and the little urchins were crying after me, one "Jesus!" another, "Hallelujah!" and a third, "There goes the Salvation Army!" I felt my soul glow with holy joy as I thought of the words, "The reproaches of them that reproached Thee fell on me."

I do not care what kind of a garb or a badge you wear,--that is not the point, but there ought to be a badge which says to every man and woman, "I belong to Jesus Christ, and I am not ashamed of my colours."

Any profession if Jesus Christ which **brings no cross** is all nonsense; it is not **confession at all**. There are plenty of Christians very brave inside their churches in the presence of their friends, or on parade. They sing:-- "Am I a soldier of the cross" or "Hold the fort, for I am coming."

I was once in a large congregation where they were singing this with the greatest gusto:-- "Wave the answer back to heaven, 'By Thy grace we will.'" I was sitting beside a warrior of the cross, one who carried the marks of many a desperate battle on his worn face. I whispered, "What should you think this people's conception of holding the fort is?" and he whispered back, "A seven-and-sixpenny pew!" Alas how true, in hundreds of instances. Are there any ministers here? If so, I ask you, Is it not **true** of three parts of your congregations? What do the people in your pews mean by holding down the fort? What fort do they hold? They hold the fort valiantly on the stock exchange, in the bank, at the office, or behind the counter. Let anybody go and try to get the better of them there, and they will hold that fort valiantly enough; but what fort are they holding for Jesus Christ? Here are two men, one is a professing Christian, the other an honourable man of the world. They are both, we will suppose, in the same business. Take their lives from day to day, and what is the difference between them? The one goes to church or chapel once or twice on Sunday. On the week day he gets up in the morning and has his breakfast, and perhaps he reads prayers out of a book, or perhaps not; this done and away he rushes to the city, to the business, where he works and thinks and plans with untiring energy till evening to make money. This is what he does six days in the week, without giving one hour per day to any kind of service to God or humanity, or even to the affairs of his own or his children's souls. The other man does just the same, only he does no go to church on Sunday, or read prayers. If you look into the lives of these two men at the end of the week, you can't find that the professed Christian has done one iota for the kingdom of God more than the other. You can't find that he has spoken to any one about his soul: he would think it out of season to talk about religion in the shop, the counting house, or on the exchange. He has never button-holed any of his acquaintances or friends in his own house; he has never knelt down by the side of any poor wandering brother or sister, never visited any sick one or prayed with the dying; he has not done a thing for the Lord Jesus, and yet he will go to chapel and sing, "Hold the fort" on Sunday, as though he had been living the life of a saint all the week. I ask, Why should such a man be called a Christian any more than his neighbour over the way? Oh, friends, it is time we wiped away this reproach, and put it out of the power of infidels and atheists to wag their heads and say, "What do ye more than the others?" It is time we drummed out of the professed armies of our Lord all such renegades or hypocrites!

Further, the great mass of these modern Christians cannot enter into this fight because they **REFUSE TO BEAR THE CONSEQUENCES**.

Fighting is hard work, whatever sort of fighting it is. You cannot fight without wounds of body, heart, or soul. You cannot be a soldier without enduring "**hardness**," and genteel Christians don't like hardness--they won't have the consequences.

First, they won't **lose their reputation**; they won't be counted fools and fanatics. I was thinking the other day, if we could have a list of the names of every person, high and low, rich and poor, who has ever been to the meetings of the Salvation Army, and who has received

~ Popular Christianity ~

light and truth, and been called and claimed by God for this war, but who has gone back into the wilderness, **what a list** that would be! And more than half of this drawing back has been because people have been ashamed to own where they got their blessing, or where they might have had it. Friends, the recording angel **keeps such a list**! A gentleman answered the other day, when bewailing his miserable spiritual condition, and one of our friends asked him to go to a holiness meeting, "**Not in my own town.**" If he had been in London, and could have crept in with the crowd into the great Congress Hall, where nobody would have recognised him, he would have gone, but **not in his own town**. That reveals the secret of thousands of people having resisted the light, and lost the blessing they might have had. It was the same spirit of false shame which prompted the question of the Pharisees, "Have any of the rulers or of the Pharisees believed on Him?"

My brother, my sister, listen:--while you care what any man or woman on earth thinks about you, or the instruments used of God to bless you, never expect to keep your blessing, for you never will. That man will go blundering on in his present lean and skeleton condition to the grave, and probably into hell, unless he repents, and finds out his mistake, and does his first works. Ashamed!--Won't be thought fanatical or weak, won't be mixed up with these common people. "Not in my own town, not in my own family,"--too proud to confess that I am not just what I should be, and that I am going amongst those poor people to be made better. Oh, dear no, not if heaven depended upon it. Listen! "Whosoever therefore shall be ashamed of Me and of My words, of him also shall the Son of Man be ashamed, when He cometh in the glory of His Father with the holy angels."

Then, further, these modern Christians refuse to **give their substance** to carry on the war.

You see war is impossible without money. I wish it were not so, but I cannot help it. This war is as impossible as any other, without money. Men and women must eat to live, however little they may manage with. And travelling expenses, rent of buildings, announcements, working expenses, prosecutions, breakdown through sickness, etc., etc., must be met. This war, I say, must have money, **AND THE MORE WAR THE MORE MONEY IS WANTED**. How many of these mongrel Christians, when faced with the needs of the war-chest, exclaim, "Money again! always begging." Now contrast the feelings of these same people when there is any great popular national war on foot. Then, what do they say in their newspapers, in their public meetings? They say to their statesmen: "You must ask for grants; you must not stick fast for money. We must win. John Bull must not be beaten for the sake of a few millions!" Ah, ah! their **hearts** are in **this** warfare! The women would sell their ornaments, and the men would hand over their balances, rather than England's freedom or greatness be sacrificed. Now then, I say that if the Christians of this London and this England of ours had the true war spirit, the spirit which says, "I want the world for Christ Jesus: I want my King to reign over the hearts of men: He shall win, be it at the cost of money or blood, or all else,"--if this spirit possessed them, instead of begrudging and reckoning how little they could give, and how much would save appearances, they would try how far they could deny themselves, and how much they could give. Oh! is this not true? Can you contradict it? Then, what am I to think of a band of professed soldiers who are always grumbling about having to give their money to extend the reign of their king, whom they profess to love more than all else besides! I do not propose to dwell on the beggarly subterfuges for getting money which these Christians resort to; it would make my cheeks crimson with shame. I said to a lady a little while ago, who was working an elaborate piece of embroidery for a bazaar, "Why don't you give the money, and use your time for something better?" She answered, "This will sell for more than it costs." "Then reckon what it will sell for and give the money; don't sit at home making other people's finery, instead of visiting the sick and seeking to save the lost!" It makes me burn with shame to think how money is raised for so-called religious purposes by semi-worldly concerts, entertainments, penny readings, and bazaars, at which there is frequently positive **gambling** to raise money for Jesus Christ, whom they say they love more than fathers, mothers, husbands, wives, houses, or lands, or anything else on earth! And these are the people who accuse the Salvation Army of want of reverence! I have sometimes talked to ladies when they have been expensively dressed, and they have said, "Really, I do not care for these things." "Then," I have said, "it is passing strange that you should be willing to spend your money for them. People generally care for the things they pay for." If Christians really cared for the reign of Jesus Christ over the hearts of men, if their hearts were set on His kingdom and on doing all they possibly could to extend it, if it were the highest

~ Popular Christianity ~

ambition of their souls, the waking and sleeping idea of their minds, do you think they would grudge to pay for it? Oh no; any child knows they would not. Such professed concern is a mockery!

Further, these modern Christians refuse to give **themselves or their children** to the propagation of the kingdom.

They studiously bring up their children from three or four years of age to eighteen or twenty, grinding it into them every day of their lives, for six and eight hours a day, how to get on and up in this world; but when Jesus Christ wants one of them--especially if he or she happens to be clever--to do any unpopular, or, in the eyes of the world, vulgar work for Him--any work that will bring a cross--they consider it absolutely throwing that child away. All the ordinary silly, sickly circles of gossip, and croquet, and drawing-room occupations, are considered most respectable and satisfactory in the case of young girls, alongside of any one of them giving herself up to seek and to save the lost. I heard a young lady say of a large circle of Christian friends: "While I was in frivolity and sin they all let me alone; I never had a letter, that I remember, from any one of them about my soul; but as soon as they found out that I had given myself to work amongst the poor and the lost, then they all woke up to a deep concern about my future, and I was flooded with letters from these **Christian friends**!" Oh! what do you think Jesus Christ would say to such people? Would He not say, as He said of their representatives, the Pharisees, "Well hath Esaias prophesied of you hypocrites, as it is written, This people honoureth me with their lips, but their heart is far from Me." Why should that daughter be thought thrown way who comes out and chooses a voluntary poverty and humility, and becomes a salvation officer to win poor lost men and women, for whom you say Jesus Christ shed His blood? If they were worth His blood, surely they are worth your daughter's respectability! Then why, because she chooses to sacrifice it, should she be put at a disadvantage compared with her elder or younger sisters, who spend their time in the frivolities of the world? Answer all ye parents, professed followers of the despised Nazarene!

Oh, the stories I could unfold, the dozens of letters that could be produced, pleading with young men and women whose hearts God has touched with pity for the perishing multitudes; bringing all the considerations of family ties, worldly position, future prospects, wealthy alliances, and I know not what else, in order to induce them to turn aside from the path of self-sacrifice and whole-hearted abandonment to the interests of the kingdom. I sometimes wonder that Christian parents and friends dare utter such words or pen such letters. I wonder that the ink does not turn red as they write, and that their accusing consciences do not force them to sign their letters "Judas."

What a different spirit parents and friends manifest with respect to their children and wards when the war-fever seizes the nation! Mothers give their sons--it may be with tears and heartaches--nevertheless ungrudgingly, to face the horrors of foreign warfare, in the shape of loneliness, toil, long marchings, exposure, privation, fever, dysentery, and a desolate death; and in other instances to wounds, loss of limbs, enfeebled constitutions, or violent death. Nay, women themselves have gone to such a war with the bravery of men, making lint, nursing the wounded, and inspiring the weak or wavering, and even working the guns; and as one rank has fallen, others have rushed to fill up the bleeding gaps. But is it so in this warfare? It used to be. No grander enthusiasm, no more heroic self-sacrifice, no more determined abandonment, has ever fired human souls than has been exhibited in the cause of Jesus Christ; but alas! it is a long while ago. The Christians of this age, as a rule, want all their time, strength, and ability, and that of their children also, to enable them to climb up the ladder of this world's social position; to get **up**, **UP**, from whence God--if Christ's teaching means anything--will say, "Thou fool!" and hurl them down to perdition when they have done.

Friends, is it not true? If so, we ought to go down on our faces and weep, and have a confession service--first, for those who feel that this truth applies to themselves; and second, for those who, although their own consciences acquit them, know that it applies to thousands round about us. Like the prophets of old did, let us humble ourselves for the sins of our people. Let us take their iniquities on our hearts as far as we may, weep over them, confess for them, and pray for them, and then set ourselves to try to arouse them up to a sense of their responsibility and danger.

Further, I charge it on the professors of popular Christianity that they have no **valour in the fight** for truth and for God.

They hold not fast the faith once delivered to the saints, but surrender first one point then another of God's revelation to any sceptical heathen who may see fit to attack it. They bid God speed alike to all professed prophets and creeds, simply because it is a matter

~ *Popular Christianity* ~

of indifference with them wither truth or error shall prevail; in fact, they are most tolerant of false teachers because they propound the easiest doctrine, often patronising the most monstrous contradictions and shameless caricatures of the gospel. There can be no doubt that millions of souls are being sacrificed to the godless, senseless antinomian gospels of the present day, gospels which have been hacked and hewed worse than any poor vivisected animal. The very standards and landmarks of goodness, truth, honesty, chastity, and godliness are broken down, and the people are taught that they have nothing to do, to sacrifice, or to suffer, in order to be saved and to get into heaven; in fact, that they can get there as easily by the broad road as by the narrow way; and all who preach the truth as Christ preached it are stigmatized as legal--as workmongers, as antichrists and papists.

Further, these modern Christians lack all **enthusiasm** in the warfare.

Look at their poor, grasping, half-hearted, uncertain profession of personal religion. They condemn anybody who dares get up and tell out any definite change that God has wrought in them, or of any glowing experience of the love, sufficiency, and power of Christ to save. They characterise all such testimony as self-exaultation and vainglory, whereas they ought to know that one of the main purposes of Christ in establishing a kingdom on the earth was that His servants might be His witnesses--not witnesses merely of His existence, but of His **power to save from sin** and its consequences. They should also study the writings of Paul, whom they claim as their great apostle, and note his bold, comprehensive, and persistent expression of his own personal experience, which occupies so large a share of his epistles.

Look at the cold, stiff, stilted public service of these modern Christians; note how they pray, sitting looking about, without reverence or decency, while their ministers pray for them by proxy; listen to their songs, mostly sung by a few dressed-up dolls perched in an organ-loft or singing-pew, doing their praises for them, perhaps with a profane or drunken leader at so much a year. Listen to the preaching,--as a rule, cold dissertations and abstractions or platitudes, "moving not a hair of the polished divine" who utters them, nor of the people who listen. An amen or hallelujah would sound almost as much out of place as it would be on the gallows! Who would ever imagine that such a minister and such worshippers were professedly serving Him of whom it was said, "He shall baptize you with the Holy Ghost with **fire**"? Alas, alas! such worshippers have nothing to be enthusiastic about. They have no personal participation in the Spirit or purposes of their professed Lord, no realization of His presence, and no glowing anticipation of His predicted triumphs. But watch the change when the time for dismissal comes; see the rush of acquaintances at the church or chapel doors to shake hands with one another; listen to the rush of tongues;--there is plenty of enthusiasm now! Frank's prizes at school or honours at college, Harry's promotion in the killing army, Gertrude's recent engagement, or Lizzie's new baby,--these are topics in which the heart is interested, and so the tongue is inspired, and the soul comes forth from its lethargy! Alas for the little children who watch the altered countenances and listen to the interested tone and manner of mother and father during the progress of these congratulations! No wonder if they conclude that **this** is the reality, and what they have been witnessing in the church or chapel is a sham. No wonder such a Christianity cannot hold its own against the forces of the enemy; no cause is so hopeless as one without enthusiasm. People who do not care much are sure to go to the wall.

Further, I charge these modern Christians with a lack of missionary enterprise.

No wonder, if they reason from the value and effect of their religion on their own characters and lives, that they do not see the importance of sending it to the heathen; and from all accounts it does no more for the heathen abroad that for the Christians at home. Alas, alas! on all these points popular Christianity must be confessed, when weighed in the balances of the sanctuary, to be found lamentably wanting.

Friends, what about yours?

The Real Warfare

We will now glance at two or three of the main characteristics of that warfare to which Christ has called His soldiers.

First: Christ's soldiers must be imbued with **the spirit** of the war.

Love to the King and concern for His interests must be the master passion of the soul. All outward effort, even that which springs from a sense of duty, will fail without this. The hardship and suffering involved in real spiritual warfare are too great for any motive but that of love. It is said that one of the soldiers of Napoleon, when being operated upon for the extraction of a bullet, exclaimed, "Cut a little deeper and you will find my general's name," meaning that it was engraven on his heart. So must the image and glory of Christ be engraven on the heart of every successful soldier of Christ. It must be the all-subduing passion of his life to bring the reign of Jesus Christ over the hearts and souls of men. A little child who has this spirit will subjugate others to his King, while the most talented and learned and active, without it, will accomplish comparatively little. If the hearts of the Christians of this generation were inspired with this spirit, and set on winning the world for God, we should soon see nations shaken to their centre, and millions of souls translated into the kingdom.

Secondly: The soldiers of Christ must be **abandoned to the war.**

They must be thoroughly committed to God's side: there can be no neutrals in this warfare. When the soldier enlists and takes the queen's shilling, he ceases to be his own property, but becomes the property of his country, must go where he is sent, stand at any post to which he is assigned, even if it be at the cannon's mouth. He gives up the ways and comforts of civilians, and goes forth with his life in his hand, in obedience to the will of his sovereign.

If I understand it, that is just what Jesus Christ demands of every one of His soldiers, and nothing less.

Some one may ask, "But we cannot all be ministers, or missionaries, or officers in the Salvation Army; must we not attend to the avocations of this life, and work for the bread that perisheth for ourselves and our families?" Certainly, but the great **end** in all we do must be the promotion of the kingdom. A man may work in order that he may eat, but he must eat to live, not to himself or for the promotion of his own purposes, but for his King, and for the advancement of His interests; and if his heart is really set on this, he will have no desire to work at his secular calling longer than is absolutely necessary to promote this object. When the necessary amount of work is done, he will gladly lay aside his implements of husbandry or handicraft for the sword of the Spirit, and for the conflict with ignorance, vice, and misery. Instead of spending his evenings in ease and self-indulgence, he will betake of himself to the streets or other places of resort for the people, and will spend what would have been his leisure hours in pressing on them the claims of God and of His truth. There will be no running away, no forsaking of the cross, no shrinking from the hard places of the field; but a determined pushing of the battle to the gate, even amid weariness, opposition, and sometimes in the face of dire defeat. I ask, Was it any less a devotion than this which actuated the martyrs and confessors of old? Have I depicted an abandonment greater than that which they understood to be their duty and privilege? If they might have drawn back, why did they persevere, many of them, through long years of conflict and persecution, culminating in stripes, imprisonment, and death? It is evident that **they** understood fidelity to Christ to involve the most perfect self-abandonment, both in life and in death.

Then, third: Christ's soldiers must **understand the tactics of war**.

In order to do this, they must make it a subject of earnest and prayerful study how to make the most of their time, talents, money, or any other resources which God may have placed at their command for the advancement of the kingdom. They must think and scheme how best to attack the enemy. Only think of the time, trouble, skill, and money that are expended by great killing armies in planning for stratagem and manoeuvre in order to surprise and overcome their enemies. Some of you will remember reading, in the records of the last German and French war, that the German officers were better acquainted with the geography of France that the French themselves; they knew every road, by-way, and field, likely to be available for their purposes. Think of the time and trouble that must have been expended in becoming thus familiar with a foreign country, and compare this with the haphazard, rule-of-thumb kind of way in which spiritual warfare is for the most part conducted. Think of the undigested schemes and abortive plans, throwing away both labour and money, embarked in by professed Christian soldiers, who have never, perhaps, spent a day's anxious thought and prayer over them in their lives. Think also of the shameful indifference--which cannot be characterised as warfare at all--of the ordinary services and arrangements of the churches. It often makes my heart ache as I pass some stately, closed-up church or chapel, with its antiquated board with a shame-faced, insignificant announcement that the "Reverend So-and-so will preach," or a "Gospel address will be delivered" at such a time on such a day; in which it is evident nothing is contemplated beyond securing the eye and attention of those who already have a liking for going to churches or chapels. And as I sometimes read the lists of meetings connected with ordinary churches, I say to myself, "As it was in the beginning, is now, and ever shall be," is evidently the creed of the originators of this programme, not with respect, perhaps, to the doctrines they preach, but with respect to the old-fashioned, effete methods by which they continue to publish them. Oh, is it not time that the professed children of light should learn, as the great Captain of our salvation exhorted them, wisdom by contrast with the children of darkness?

As I heard some friends talking the other day about the rescue of Gordon, and listened to their calculations as to the probably cost being some millions of money, and perhaps thousands of lives, I could not help thinking, yes, and I suppose all England (the Christians included) will think this quite a legitimate expenditure of both money and life to rescue this one man and the little band who is with him; and yet, if we were to ask for a few millions of money, and propose to sacrifice a few hundreds of lives in the rescue of millions of the human race from a bondage of misery and destruction ten thousand times more appalling than that which threatens General Gordon, they would call us mad enthusiasts and senseless fanatics. Alas, alas! we may well ask, Where is the zeal of the Christians of this generation for the Lord of hosts? How much do they care about His reign over the hearts of their fellow-men? What is their appreciation of the present and eternal benefits embraced in His salvation; or what is their estimate of the "crown of life" which He promises to give to every one of His conquering soldiers?

Fourth: The soldiers of Christ must **believe in victory**.

Faith in victory is an indispensable condition to successful warfare of any kind. It is universally recognised by generals of killing armies, that if the enthusiasm of expected conquest be destroyed, and their troops imbued with fear and doubt as to the ultimate result, defeat is all but certain. This is equally true with respect to spiritual warfare, hence the repeated and comprehensive assurance and promises of victory from the great Captain of our salvation.

The true soldier of Christ, who has the spirit of the war and who is abandoned to its interests, has an earnest in his soul of coming victory. He knows it is only a question of time, **and time is nothing to love!** As he is lying in the trenches, or taking long marches, or suffering for the want of common necessaries, or enduring the sharpest bayonets or heaviest fire of the enemy, or lying wounded, overcome by fatigue, pressed by discouragement, realizing the greatness of the conflict in contrast with his own weakness--in the very darkest hours and severest straits, he has the herald of coming victory sounding in his ears. The faithful soldier **knows** that he shall win, and that his King will ultimately reign, not only over a few, but over all the kingdoms of this earth, and that He must reign till He has put all enemies under His feet. This faith inspires him to endure hardship and to suffer loss, to hold on. He never thinks of turning his back to the foe, or shirking the cross, or turning the stones into bread, or of trying to shorten the march. He never thinks of withdrawing from the thick of the fight, but goes on through perils by land, by sea, by his own countrymen, but the heathen, by false brethren at home and abroad. He looks onward through the dark clouds to the proud moment when the King will say, "Well done, good and faithful servant!" He listens, and above the din of the earthly conflict he hears the words, "Be thou faithful unto death, and I will give thee a crown of life!"

LECTURE V

THE SHAM JUDGMENT IN CONTRAST WITH THE GREAT THRONE

The Sham Judgment

MANY people dislike the very sound of the word judgment. They have abandoned, as far as they can, any belief in a judgment to come, and they ignore as uncharitable and severe any expression of judgment as to the doings and characters of individuals in the present; but somehow the instincts of humanity are too strong for them, and these very people find themselves, in spite of their theories, pronouncing judgment both on themselves and others every day of their lives.

God has reared a judgment seat in every man's conscience, which in some slight measure answers to, and prefigures the sentence which He declares He will pronounce in every man's action, whether it be good or bad.

Then if there be a great Judge of all, and a standard of right and wrong which He has set up, it must be of supreme importance that we should correctly understand what this standard is, and that we should judge of the conduct of ourselves and of those around us according to it. Surely nothing could be more deceptive and soul-ruining than to accept as correct any short of the one unalterable and eternal standard of righteousness and truth which He has laid down; and yet, alas! popular Christianity distinguishes itself by nothing more than by a systematic misrepresentation of right and wrong, calling evil good and good evil. Just as in the days of Christ the spirit and essence of the law of God was set aside and made of no effect by traditional interpretations of the letter, so in our time interpretations and expositions, in direct antagonism to the plainest words of Christ, are palmed upon the world by many of the official representatives of Christianity, who back up their false tenets by quotations from "the word," separated from their explanatory connections, and made to sanction views and practices the very opposite to the mind and intention of their Divine Author.

In pointing out as plainly as I am able a few of these misrepresentations, I know only too well I shall lay myself open to criticism, and that I may even run the risk of wounding some hearts that I would fain cheer. But the vital importance of the subject will not permit me to pass it over lightly.

First: "Judge not that ye be not judged" is one of the favorite texts of popular Christianity, which is interpreted to mean that we are on no account to form an opinion of the rightness or wrongness of anybody's conduct. Under the specious guise of charity, faith and unbelief, obedience to God and disobedience, sin and holiness, are to be confounded in one indiscriminate hodge-podge, and their actors and abettors treated exactly alike, making no separation between the precious and the vile.

This spurious charity is pushed to such an extent that even the man who has pledged himself to preach certain doctrines, and who is actually employed as the agent of a Church for so doing, is not to be condemned if his "riper judgment" should lead him to renounce those doctrines; while at the same time he holds fast the salary and position with which he was entrusted in view of his original engagement.

On the same principle we are asked to allow that people who never go to a place of worship or bow their knees in prayer may be as good and faithful servants of God as any others. We are told that perhaps they are carrying out "the Divine will in a spirit of true devotion to duty," that working is praying, and that a man's belief bounds his responsibility, and so forth.

"We are all aiming at the same thing" is a favourite way of expressing this popular Christianity, which just suits the ideas of drunkards, adulterers, and liars, as well as of shallow professors.

To declare positively that people are sinners, condemned already, and on their way to hell, is accounted as "uncharitable judging," "really dreadful," and no one, we are told, can possibly be justified in coming to such a conclusion.

All this we could understand perfectly, coming from the camps of infidelity or from the haunts of vice; but to find it passed off in connection with the name and teachings of Jesus Christ is monstrous indeed. What a sham to worship Him who declares Himself to be **THE** Way, the Truth, and the Life, if there be no certain way, no definable difference between the true and the false, no practical separation between the Christ life and the life without Christ! Surely it is high time for all who care about the reign of Christ on the earth to make up their minds to one thing or the other. If Christ be our Master, let us learn His lessons, and abide by His rule, and obey His commands. If, on the other hand, some are unwilling to see any difference between the narrow and the broad road, between those who are in the kingdom of God or out of it, who are with Christ or against Him, let them be honest enough to declare openly that they have no Christ and will have no prophet by "Society."

Another text which might be taken as setting forth a very favourite theory of modern Christianity is that in which Paul personified the struggles of a convicted but unsaved soul: "For the good that I would I do not: but the evil which I would not, that I do." We are all to look upon ourselves as "poor, incapable, fallible creatures," and this assumed humility is to absolve us from all condemnation, on account either of doing evil or neglecting to do good. Instead of condemning ourselves and others, when convicted of some flagrant wrong or manifest inconsistency, we are to look upon it as only what might have been expected. How often have I heard people say, with regard to some man holding an official position in the Church, "Well, he does not do this, that, or the other (whatever may be the duty in question) as he might; but, you know, he can't do everything." Such an apology as this would be beautiful in the extreme, applied to those who are known to be earnestly and faithfully striving to do their share for the extension of the kingdom of God; but when applied, as I have generally heard it, to what every one knows to be a systematic and inexcusable neglect of everyday duty, it is no more nor less than a wholesale cloaking of sin. But, friends, whatever you do, never allow your minds for a moment to trifle with questions of duty, for nothing can be more fatal to either body or soul than to give way to the theory that one really cannot be expected to do what one ought.

How differently people treat this question of doing their duty in commercial matters. Imagine that business man who cannot attend to **all** his customers, or who thinks it unnecessary to keep his place of business open all the week and **every** week. What would you think of a servant who should consider it unreasonable to get up at the proper time **every** morning, or carry out your wishes in matters in which her views differed from yours? How long could society hang together if this looseness of thought as to what we ought and ought not to do were permitted to enter into the sphere of every day life? But alas, alas! how much more ruinous is this looseness when it relates to our great spiritual duties towards God and our fellow-creatures. Either you ought or you ought not always to pray and not to faint--to learn and to do the will of God, to care for perishing souls, to warn, counsel, and help those around you; and what applies to you applies to all who take upon them the name of Christ in any way whatever. We should never, on any account, allow ourselves to excuse any neglect of God and duty, because such neglect is all but universal, but we should look at things as they are, and in the light of the judgment throne; and when we see conduct worthy of condemnation, condemn it, and be determined to separate ourselves in heart and life from evil practices, however much respected they may be, and to take our stand on the side of duty and of God at all costs.

I tell you honestly that I have turned away numberless times of late years, and with almost despairing disgust, from audiences of what would be called intelligent Christians, that is to say, persons who talk and act upon an intelligent view of any imaginable subject, except that of Christian duty. How often do I hear the remark, "We know things are not as they should be," from people who have not the slightest intention of striving in any way to make things better, and who would not, on any account, incur the odium of expressing any condemnation of that neglect of religious duty which they profess so much to deplore. Away with this unmanly, unwomanly cowardice. We have the light; let us come to it in order to see whether our deeds, and the deeds of those around us who profess to be "working for God," are wrought in Him. We can, by God's grace, do our duty, if we will. As we tried to show in a former lecture, Christ came on purpose to empower us to do it; but let those who will not have such a doctrine and such a Christ, but who prefer to accept the miserable theories of impotency, which would not be tolerated for a moment in the kitchen, the shop, or the exchange,-- let them at least save Christ from the indignity of having such helpless, incapable creatures called by His name, and professing to be His followers. He says with respect to all such, "Why call ye **Me**, Lord, Lord, and do not the things that I say?"

"**But the Lord looks at the heart**," is another of the pet doctrines of popular Christianity.

True, terribly true in the right sense,--for God is not to be mocked with lip service or the formality of worship in which the heart has no

~ Popular Christianity ~

share,--but false, ruinously false, when it means, as it generally does, that all sorts of wrong may be passed over and excused, if people only say they mean to do right.

I rejoice beyond all expression in the precious thought of the Lord's long suffering and tender mercy towards those who sit in darkness; and if we were living in the centre of Africa, where people have been trained only to fear and worship some hideous imaginary power of evil,--if we had absolutely no spirit of truth, and no word of light to hear of to read, no knowledge of God or a Saviour,--it might be admissible to consider everybody right who meant right; but even those in this country who are most sceptical as to Divine revelation cannot pretend to be in any such position as this, much less people who profess to call themselves Christians. Is there anybody here taking refuge in this hollow subterfuge? Friend, let me ask you, did you really worship and serve God last Sunday? Had you any convictions as to what He wished you to do, not only on that day but throughout the following week? If so, have you acted on them, have you honestly tried to carry them out? If not, do not, I beseech you, try to pacify your conscience with any silly nonsense about the Lord looking at the heart. He has plainly told us over and over again in the New Testament, and in the very last book of it, that He will judge every man according to **his works**, and, moreover, He has laid down the same rule of judgment for us. "By their fruits ye shall know them." "Little children, let no man deceive you: he that doeth righteousness is righteous." I fear there are thousands of professed Christians excusing themselves from the performance of the most manifest duty by this excuse; for instance, when a prayer meeting is announced, there are a certain number of people who make an effort to be present, but a much larger number of so-called Christians who deliberately choose to keep away. It is quite allowable to apply the doctrine of the Lord's looking at the heart to the poor mother who would fain be there, were she not detained by the inexorable claims of half a dozen little children; but to cloak over with the same excuse, the constant indifference, nay, positive irreligion, in the great majority, is only to refuse to come to the light because it would condemn you. People who mean well, where there is no physical impossibility in the way, **do well**; but those who fail to do well, will fare ill when the great reckoning day comes.

Further, I charge it upon popular Christianity, even when it does pay some tribute to the truth with regard to character, by recognising here and there what it calls an "excellent man," or a "noble woman," that when you come to examine into the meaning of these phrases, they are, in many instances, utterly misleading. Most generally the persons thus eulogised are distinguished, rather than for lack of those peculiar characteristics set forth by Christ and His apostles as of supreme importance, than by the possession of them. Just try to call up a person so distinguished within your own knowledge, and ask yourself how they have earned their title. To begin with, do they excel in prayer, or are they in most cases persons who were never known to pray in public, or, at any rate, without being specially called upon to do so? Or, are they renowned for praying by the bedsides of the sick, or even with their own families in the privacy of their own homes? Do these persons excel in faith, shown by their works in the way of bold, straightforward testimony for God, or in daring, unpopular enterprises for the salvation of men? or are they generally silent both in public and private, giving no personal testimony as to their knowledge of Christ, and carefully abstaining from any outward demonstration on His behalf, which would bring them into discredit with their neighbors? Probably they do excel in what is called charity; but is not this generally due to the fact that they are much richer than others, and only out of their enormous abundance do they contribute occasionally large sums for Christian or philanthropic objects. What a name may be acquired in modern Christendom by the judicious use of a few hundred pounds per year, without so much as speaking a kind word to a brother or sister in need, or denying yourself a moment's ease or a single luxury! It is not notorious that in ninety-nine cases out of a hundred it is simply the possession of a certain amount of wealth which gives a man or woman his or her grade in religious as well as in civil society, and that people chosen for and entrusted with leading positions in churches, are simply those who have the best houses of their own? By-and-by their splendid coffins will be pompously deposited in the family vault, and you will be told that they "maintained an unblemished character for many years;" that is to say, they neither got drunk, blasphemed, committed robbery, nor picked anybody's pocket. They lived in society in such a style as made them welcome in the circles of semi-worldliness everywhere. Their linen and their dresses were unblemished, for they never turned aside, like their Divine Master, into any of the soiling habitations of the poor and the wretched, nor mingled amongst such mobs as continually jostled Him all the way through life. Their names were always mentioned with honour, for they took care never to let them be used in connection with any enterprise, even on behalf of Jesus Christ, which was not considered "quite the thing."

Do not misunderstand me. I am very far from wishing to pour contempt upon such persons, for without them what would become of the churches and of benevolent enterprises generally? I do not question that many of these individuals have at one time or other been converted, and might have become true saints, had they been faithfully dealt with; but alas! they have, to a great extent, been made the victims of that sham judgment which now selects them as its standard-bearers. Of many of them, I doubt not, it might be written, were Jesus Christ again among us, and were they brought in contact with Him, that He looked upon them and loved them, notwithstanding all their worldliness and pride of position. But what I want to point out is, that such persons are not distinguished by popular Christianity for the peculiarly Christ-like traits in their characters, but for the possession and use of a long purse. This exaltation of mere morality with money stamps modern Christianity as an **unjust judge**, and it will be fatal to your views of what Christ demands of you, if you accept its model men and women as the representatives of Christian excellence.

Fifth: As I have before remarked, there has come over society of late quite a fever of professed benevolence towards the poor; and yet, in connection with this very pleasing awakening to the existence of millions of miserable people, we have another striking illustration of the sham judgment of modern Christendom. "Those wretched, filthy people" are simply the poorer classes, who are compelled by their poverty to herd together by families in small rooms, surrounding perhaps a court-yard full of oyster-shells and other refuse, at which society--and Christian society, too--turns up its nose, and declares that the people breathe an "atmosphere of moral pollution." Perfectly true; there is an atmosphere of moral pollution present in these dark alleys and horrible dens, to which people are driven by thousands, that others may have plenty of room in which to carry out their ideas of civilisation; but to eyes that look at things in the light of God, I say there is an atmosphere of moral pollution, not a wit less dangerous, and far more blameworthy, in very different circles.

Is it not notorious that multitudes of people amongst what are called the higher classes deliberately denude themselves of ordinary clothing, and then go in a half-dressed condition, with every addition of ornament that can be conceived, to insure that they shall be noticed and admired, to large places of public amusement? Is there not a growing disposition in Christian circles to look upon it as perfectly harmless for Christian families, including often those of ministers, to spend hours together, dressed in the way I have described, at parties, balls, and other entertainments, frequently given within the precinct of some consecrated building, or in order to raise money for church purposes? Now, I ask, how it come to pass that the poor are spoken of as herding together without regard for decency, under the circumstances of necessity which I have described; while the herding together of the rich and well-to-do in this voluntary indecency should be regraded with complacency and described are refined and genteel? That such is the judgment of modern Christendom can only be attributed to one fact--the power of the purse; and that the Churches should in the main devote their attention to the well-to-do classes, while they regard the masses of the people as a kind of outside element, to be operated upon by separate agencies, as a few missionaries and Bible-women, is, I contend, a crying scandal to the Saviour's name. The judgment of Jesus Christ led Him to spend most of His time herding with fishermen, with publicans and sinners. Their language might often be very violent and bad, and their home life simply scandalous; but the Son of God preferred to make His bed in a fishing-boat, and to sit talking with that infamous woman of Samaria, rather than to hobnob with the religious swelldom of Jerusalem, the outside of whose cup and platter would have passed muster with modern Christianity, whilst their lives were full of hypocrisy and unrighteousness.

Sixth: "The brutal tastes of the lower orders" is another pet phrase of modern Christendom.

It represents the idea that for a poor man, who has to keep himself and his family on a few shillings per week by hard labour, which takes away all inclination towards study or more exalted pursuits, it is a brutal taste to like to have a quart of fourpenny beer as often as his scanty means will allow. It is a brutal taste to take pleasure in seeing two men fight each other, with their fists inflicting in the course of half an hour many hard knocks and bruises; and it is a still ore brutal taste which leads men to train animals to fight each other, and to take pleasure in seeing them do so. Now I perfectly concur in the

~ Popular Christianity ~

denunciation of all these evils, from which God is enabling the Salvation Army to rescue multitudes of these poor, so-called "brutal fellows;" but let us turn the light of truth upon the Christian society which shrugs its shoulders in horror at the mere description of these men who get drunk and beat their wives; the Christian society whose refined taste leads it to have as little intercourse as possible with these lower orders.

What sort of taste is it, which, in the presence of the existing state of things among the poor, spends not fourpence but four shillings, and double and treble that sum on a single bottle of wine for the jovial entertainment of a few friends, and from twenty to forty pounds for a dinner to be swallowed by a dozen or two of people? I maintain that no splendid furniture, no well-trained and liveried servants, no costly pictures or display of finery or jewels, can redeem such a scene, viewed in the light of the teachings of Christ, from being worthy of being called "brutal," and all the more brutal because it is delighted in by persons whose intelligence and knowledge of the awful state of things in the world around them must make them fully aware of the good that might be done with the money which they thus lavish upon their lusts.

Let me take you to another scene. Here is His Grace, the Duke of Rackrent, and the Right Honourable Woman Seducer, Fitz-Shameless; and the gallant Colonel Swearer, with half the aristocracy of a county, male and female, mounted on horses worth hundreds of pounds each, and which have been bred and trained at a cost of hundreds more, and what for? "This splendid field" are waiting whilst a poor little timid animal is let loose from confinement and permitted to fly in terror from its strange surroundings. Observe the delight of all the gentlemen and noble ladies when a while pack of strong dogs is let loose in pursuit, and then behold the noble chase! The regiment of well-mounted cavalry and the pack of hounds all charge at full gallop after the poor frightened little creature. It will be a great disappointment if by any means it should escape, or be killed within as short a time as an hour. The sport will be excellent in proportion to the time during which the poor thing's agony is prolonged, and the number of miles it is able to run in terror of its life. Brutality! I tell you, that in my judgment, at any rate, you can find nothing in the vilest back slums, more utterly, more deliberately, more savagely cruel that all that; and yet this is a comparatively small thing. One of the greatest employments of every

Christian government and community is to train thousands of men, not to fight with their fists only, in the way of inflicting a few passing sores, but with weapons capable, it may be, of killing human beings at the rate of so many per minute. It is quite a "scientific taste" to study how to destroy a large vessel with several hundreds of men on board instantaneously. Talk of brutality! Is there anything half as brutal as this within the whole range of rowdyism? But against all this, modern Christianity, which professed to believe the teaching of Him who taught us not to resist evil, but to love our enemies, and to treat with the utmost benevolence hostile nations, has nothing to say. All the devilish animosity, hard-hearted cruelty, and harrowing consequences of modern warfare, are not only sanctioned but held up as an indispensable necessity of civilised life, and in times of war, patronized and prayed for in our churches and chapels, with as much impudent assurance as though Jesus Christ had taught, "But I say unto you, an eye for an eye, a tooth for a tooth, and, return evil for evil, hate your enemies and pursue them with all the diabolical appliances of destruction which the devil can enable you to invent." Alas, alas! is it not too patent for intelligent contradiction that the most detestable and brutal think in the judgment of popular Christianity is not brutality, cruelty, or injustice, but **poverty and vulgarity**? With plenty of money you may pile up your life with iniquities, and yet be blamed, if blamed at all, only in the mildest terms, whereas one flagrant act of sin in a poor and illiterate person is enough to stamp him, with the majority of Christians, as a creature from whom they would rather keep at a distance. I had an amusing corroboration of this the other day from one of my younger daughters who had been visiting a poor criminal in one of our large prisons. She said to one of the officers in attendance, "I suppose you do not often have rich people in here?" he replied, "No, miss, we very seldom get anybody but poor folks," and on her replying, "No, I am afraid it is because you do not look out so sharply for them," he remarked to a fellow officer, "She's all there."

Seventh: Further, "the criminal classes" is another of the cant phrases of modern Christianity, which thus brands every poor lad who steals, because he is hungry, but stands, hat in hand, before the rich man whose trade is well known to be a system of wholesale cheatery.

It is never convenient for ministers or responsible churchwardens or deacons to ask how Mr. Money-maker gets the golden sovereigns or crisp notes which look so well in the collection. He may be the most "accursed sweater" who ever waxed fat on that murderous cheap needlework system, which is slowly destroying the bodies and ruining the souls of thousands of poor women, both in this and other "civilised" countries. He may keep scores of employées standing wearily sixteen hours per day behind the counter, across which they dare not speak the truth, and on salaries so small that all hope of marriage and home is denied to them. Or he may trade in some damning thing which robs men of all that is good in this world and all hope for the next, such as opium or intoxicating drinks; but if you were simple enough to suppose that modern Christianity would object to him on account of any of these things,--in fact, that you were alluding to such as he, in the phrase "criminal classes,"--how respectable Christians would open their eyes, and, in fact, suspect that you had recently made your escape from some lunatic asylum, and ought to be hastened back there as soon as possible. If any one should dare to case any reflections upon any of these Christian money-makers, the representatives of their churches would say, "Hush, hush, my dear sir, Mr. So-and-so is the great man at our place, you know; they would be glad enough of him at the church opposite, but he likes our minister, and we mean to propose him as a deacon at the next church meeting." So the wholesale and successful thief is glossed over and called by all manner of respectable names by the representatives of a bastard Christianity. It is ready enough to cry, Stop, thief, when some poor fellow who has been out of work for perhaps months, gets desperate at the sight of children crying for bread, and makes a bungling attempt at getting what is not his own in order to satisfy them; or when it hears that such men, left helplessly to their own devices, take to living together, and bringing up a generation of thieves, it cries out vigorously against the criminals. Sure, it may suggest a mission to them, and even set about it in a helpless patronising sort of way, wondering if really it is of any use to try to help "such men," as though they were of different flesh and blood to themselves. Verily such Christianity **is** of different blood from Him who preferred talking to a thief in His own last moments, to holding conversation with any priest of white-washed temple worshipper standing around. The man who hung by His side was a great ruffian, no doubt, but then he had been trained in that way; and if we want the judgment of Jesus Christ on such a point, He would certainly give it against the pet of modern Christianity, and in favour of this poor rough. The man whom Jesus

Christ consigned to a hopeless perdition was he who made long prayers, and at the same time devoured widows' houses; or whose barns were filled with plenty while Lazarus lay covered with sores at his gates.

On no point does the sham judgment of popular Christianity appear more startlingly in contrast with that of Jesus Christ, than on the every-day question of honesty. It knows that its rich tradesmen are so dishonest in their modes of carrying on their business, that if some poor fellow comes out of prison, determined to do right and earn his bread honestly, we know scarcely any with whom we dare entrust him, and with whom he would not be tempted to break his resolution, by being asked to tell business lies, or perform business tricks, which to his "unchristianised" intelligence is only another mode of thieving; but Christianity goes on, with virtuous breath declaring that the poor and found-out thieves are criminals, while the rich and secret scoundrels are the valued supporters of her institutions.

Further: "Desecrating the Sabbath" is another virtuous-sounding phrase, which is accepted as the expression of a very reverential religion. So it should be, bet here the sham judgment comes in again! What **is** desecrating the Sabbath? Well, it is not dressing up on fabulously costly clothes (sometimes unpaid for), as near in fabric, style, and fashion as can be to those worn in the very vilest services of sin. It is not to lie in bed consuming the early hours of the day, and then to flaunt in this array to one short service, as an exhibition of self and respectability, spending the remainder of the "sacred day" in an easy chair with the last new book. This is Sabbath **keeping**, even though to carry it out comfortably, servants may have to work over an elaborate dinner, or the turning out of a luxuriant equipage. Then what is "desecrating"? Well, go and spend next Sunday evening in Mr. Easy's mansion, and he will show you. You will not have an unpleasant time, that is, if your notions agree with his. He will give you a splendid meal, and then you will be allowed to lounge on one of his soft couches, while your host tells you spicy stories about the popular ministers of his denomination, or his daughter will play to you some "sacred" music on the piano or the harp. Fire and lamp-light will gleam softly, and thick curtains shut out the night, about which some one will occasionally remark that it is "awful weather."

Presently a harsh, discordant sound is heard, like shouting and singing with some brass instrumental music all mixed up; and if you

~ Popular Christianity ~

looked out you would see a little handful of men and women, wet and mud-stained, nearly exhausted in the struggle with rain and storm, and the half rough, half good-natured crowd, who have been allured out of yonder alley, and are now going, swearing, pushing, rolling along, on a fashion of their own, to a little room, or a low music-hall, where these tambourine players and the rest do congregate. Your host will jump up with an annoyed air, and exclaim with great emphasis, "Desecrating the Sabbath, that is what I call it!" and he will go on to expound his views until you understand that it is a Sabbath breaking for those poor folks to have made a noise in the street, even though they were only doing what David and Jesus Christ insisted was to be done--praising God with a loud voice, and confessing Him before all men. For, "Blessed be the name of the Lord!" or "Glory! hallelujah!" certainly had rung clearly out above the din with almost tragic earnestness. You will learn that your host's son and daughter have kept the Sabbath by singing in the church choir, although you see them later on, the one reading a novel, the other strolling out of the house with a cigar and a hint about returning with the latch-key. Now I charge it upon popular Christianity that its professors know all the miserable desecration which lies under the while modern keeping of the day, and yet have not courage to condemn, but keep their blame for some effort to serve the Lord which they deem vulgar and distasteful. Modern Christendom gives its judgment in favour of the hollow, conventional sacredness of the performance of the dressed-up choir, whose very manner and countenance often betray the irreligion and frivolity of their hearts, and which neither wins the souls of sinners nor stirs the souls of saints; but reserves its strongest censure for the unscientific, rough-and-ready brass band, which empties the public-houses and gets sinners saved by scores and hundreds.

Further: "The Sanctuary," according to modern Christian theories, is a "holy place," and yet a place where no one must speak of being now and actually holy! In fact, it is a place where scarcely anybody except the minister may say a word to, or for God; where such a scene as that recorded in 1 Cor. xiv. 23-31 would be counted the highest fanaticism, and next door to blasphemy. I have heard of a congregation being actually thrown into dismay by the cry to God for mercy of some poor sinner who had been previously convicted, and gone to that chapel in the hope of finding the way of salvation; but he had a near escape of being ejected by the beadle. Better everybody refrain their feet from going to these modern sanctuaries, that have a crowd of rough, needy sinners really wanting light and needing to be brought to repentance and salvation. "Keep silence before me," says modern Christian society, and not a word is breathed to hurt its feelings. It is a literal fact that in these modern sanctuaries any manifestation of the **LIVING GOD** is the last thing expected or desired. Imagine the scare and horror of excitement and the intense surprise if He came, as He did once in an upper room, with His baptism of fire, in the middle of one of these quiet and soothing services next Sunday morning! There would be a quicker and more precipitous exit of many of the professed worshippers than there was from the temple when He drove them out with a scourge of small cords! The great work nearest to **His heart**-- the gathering in of the poor, the maimed, the halt, and the blind, or the victims of sin, debauchery, and crime, the thieves and the harlots--is the very last thing desired and expected in these modern sanctuaries. That He should speak in what is called His own "house" is the last thing arranged for. Alas, alas! do not these facts prove that these are the temples of Mammon, of respectability, or miserable, hollow, Pharisaic profession, where all manner of ungodliness is glossed over by what answers to the tithing of mint, anise, and cummin? and yet Christianity baptises these temples with her name, and holds up to ridicule and contempt the open-air ring, where poor, simple, but devout and consecrated people, plead with God to speak, and try to make the world hear His message.

Further: "He is much to be condemned!"

What for?

Never, as we have shown, because he is taking it too easy; never because he is enjoying a thousand a year, and letting men go on in sin undisturbed; never because he makes no straightforward, bold confession of Christ, or takes not up the cross to follow Him; never because he does not deny himself even the luxuries indulged by others in his "position," in order that he may push on the interests of the kingdom of God in the world!! "But **he** is much to be condemned" who gets into trouble,--into a row, as it is politely termed,--for Christ's sake. Modern Christians ask with bated breath, "Why ever should he have gone and stirred up the moral cesspools all around him, filling the atmosphere with 'moral pollution'? How could he be so quixotic and fanatical as to expect to make things better where the bishops and clergy, and all the most influential food people of the day, had long decided that it was a better left alone? We really cannot pity him," say these modern Christians, "if he is set upon and traduced and persecuted by all the libertines and whoremongers of the age; we fear that he is seeking notoriety, and posing to be a martyr!!" And thus this bastard Christianity adds its bann to the curses of God's enemies on the man who has **not** done well for himself, but who has dared to stand up for the poor and helpless, for broken-hearted mothers and fathers, and for the innocent and infant victims of the devils of lust and villainy, incarnate in the persons of rich debauchees. Modern Christianity has got rid to a great extent of damnation, but it can damn right vigorously in its own fashion all those who "go to extremes." It can pour its half-sneering contempt upon ignorant, blundering fishermen or mechanics, but who, nevertheless, love God and souls, and believe in heaven and hell, and who really exercise self-denial and take trouble in order to serve God and save men. If such men go to prison to win some point for God and liberty of conscience, these Christians say in their drawing-rooms, in their magazines and newspapers, "Ah, they are trying to become notorious! they are zealous of being thought martyrs!" And thus they join hands, as of old, with those who stood around the cross and wagged their heads, and said, "He saved others, Himself He cannot save"; and they can pronounce this judgment with such a pious, ex-cathedrâ air that many simple men accept it as really the judgment of Christ's body on earth, instead of the hollow, sham verdict of modern Pharisees.

In conclusion, let me repeat that if my words seem to condemn the great majority of the representatives of Christianity around us, it is with sincere grief that I admit it. Would to God there were few localities, few churches, and few ministers to which my remarks could be applied! But if there be not few but many, I cannot help it. I appeal to you whether I have spoken more than the truth; and I speak it in love of it. I would gladly forbear to speak out thus,--I have forborne for long, and have frequently felt condemned in so doing, and it is only because I see the utter hopelessness of any improvement, of any recurrence to the simplicity and purity of the gospel, without an utter abandonment of the false and hollow judgment of modern Christianity with respect to the matters we have been reviewing, that I venture to speak thus. I would fain hope that some of you may be induced to forsake every refuge of lies which has been reared around you, and to abandon all the false standards of faith and practice to which I have alluded, and open your hearts and ears to listen to the voice that never changes, but which in all ages alike tells men of a just judgment to come. We must all appear before the judgment-seat of Christ; and it will be no excuse for us there that we were surrounded by false witnesses, sham lights, and an openly received system of hypocrisy. God has shown us His beloved Moses, Daniels, Nehemiahs, Jeremiahs, Pauls, Johns, and numberless other worthies, standing out gloriously alone in the midst of a Pagan society, full of refined and splendid iniquity, and standing out ever more Divine, when all around were "weighed in the balances and found wanting." You have but the old choice to make; may God enable you to make it, and to stand out for God and righteousness against all around you.

The Judgment of the Great White Throne

As we remarked in the first part of this lecture, the innate convictions of humanity are too strong for the successful annihilation of a dread of coming judgment. It seems to have been the universal opinion of the wisest and best of the human race that there **ought** to be a judgment. The continual miscarriage of justice in this world, and the unequal distribution of its goods and enjoyments; its false standard of right and wrong; its unjust and sham judgments, to which we have already alluded, have seemed to drive it in upon the reason of all thoughtful beings that there must come a settling day.

The unavenged wrongs of multitudes of the poor and the oppressed; of millions of slaves; of poor, helpless children; of tens of thousands of poor, broken-hearted girls,--mere children,--who have been wrecked of virtue and happiness through the vice of those double or treble their age, and who were fully awake to the consequences of their conduct;--wrongs such as these, and multitudes of others, all unjudged and unrequited in this world, seem to demand some future retribution. The unpunished sins of multitudes who have flourished in their lives and gone in triumph to their graves, who floated to their positions of eminence, fame, and luxury through the tears and blood of widows, orphans and others, down-trodden by their greed and power, cry from the ground, as did the blood of Abel, for avenging justice.

Methinks if we could face this guilty crowd and compel them to speak, they would be obliged to say, "Yes, during our lives we violated all law and justice, won the applause of men and the pleasures and

~ Popular Christianity ~

honours in which we revelled by means of the sorrows and suffering of our fellows; but no strong arm stayed our progress, no tongue denounced our villainies, no power punished our crimes; we lived and fattened, and died with the approbation, nay, applause, of men ringing in our ears; and after death we were praised and flattered on tablets of marble, in newspapers and biographies, as though we had been the excellent of the earth. We know that we are of the devil; we expect and are waiting for the judgment."

Further, the common-sense of humanity perceives that human lives are all unfinished at the grave, and require some appendix, some explanation. If you found a book with the story all unfinished,--the villains and seducers all unpunished, and the poor, down-trodden slaves unavenged, the wronged and helpless people undelivered,--you would feel that there must be another volume somewhere. So, when life breaks up, with almost all men there are so many things and doings and feelings all unfinished, that you might write on every grave-stone, "To be continued in the next world." It is as if the tree were blighted at its bloom; as if the life were sapped at its source; as if the flood were turned back as its tide.

But, as we have already noted, there is a judgment already begun here and now. The same Divinity is at work in this world who will reign and operate in the next, and He is working on precisely the same principles. The moral government of this world is going on under the shadow, so to speak, of the great white throne. The shadow of that tribunal is reflected on all the tribunals and transactions of this earth.

Formerly, when the judges visited the provincial towns, there used to be a sort of public entry. The legal civic dignitaries went forth to meet them and march in procession with them into town, preceded by heralds with trumpets, announcing the coming of judgment for the wrong-doers of those towns. So God has His heralds abroad in the world, proclaiming that He is coming. These heralds are already gone forth; they are here to-day.

There is a herald in every man's heart, giving foretastes of what the judgment will be, pointing out and convicting him of sin.

Every transgressor of the Divine law stands condemned before his own judgment seat. Conscience pronounces sentence on him according to his works, independently of all creeds and theories. A false gospel, under the auspices of popular Christianity, essays to set at nought this judgment, and to tell men that they are not to judge themselves according to their works, but according to their beliefs. But God's herald in them remorselessly holds up their sin, and points to coming retribution. Conscience asserts itself, and the man who has sinned knows, feels that he must be judged.

Further, not only does conscience convict of sin, but to a certain extent **punishes** sin, even here. What horrors men suffer from their guilty consciences, in spite of all their infidel reasonings and hopes. How many suicides will be found, like Judas, to have been driven to distraction by the remorse and anguish of realized guilt. Is not the fact that such suffering is the consequence of sin unquestionable evidence that so long as the soul continues to live and remain guilty, it must continue to suffer? If transgressors can find no comfort or deliverance from this tormenting sense of guilt in this world, on what principle can it be argued that they will find it in the next? If conscience is too strong for them here, what ground is there for supporting that they will rise superior to it in the future?

Secondly: God has a herald in society. We have wandered a long distance from God in these days, I admit, and as distance from the sun brings corresponding darkness and obliterates the distinctions between natural objects, so distance from God brings spiritual darkness and induces blindness to moral distinctions. Nevertheless, far as society has for away from God, and rotten as it largely is, still it has the herald trumpet blowing loudly enough to proclaim evil to **be evil**, and, being evil, to be amenable to judgment. And although many preachers of a false theology, under the patronage of popular Christianity, combine to persuade men and themselves that they will escape punishment, the very libertines, thieves, gamblers, and moral bankrupts of all descriptions, pronounce their judgment to be false, saying, "Hypocrites all of you, we know we are of the devil; his works we do, and we expect to go to hell."

I have no doubt that the great secret of the success of the Salvation Army with multitudes of the openly wicked and profane is that we go straight to their consciences, attacking their sins, making no excuse or palliation, but telling them as straight as Jesus Christ Himself told the sinners of His day, that, except they repent, forsake their sins, and turn to God, everlasting fire must be their portion. This gospel answers to the voice of conscience within; they know it is true, because it matches their most secret and powerful intuitions, whereas the popular gospel of this day, its judgment included, is the laughing-stock of hell; it dare neither damn the sinner nor sanctify the saint.

~ Popular Christianity ~

But we must now consider for a few minutes what the character of this judgment is to be, which is proclaimed alike by conscience, reason, and religion. And the **BIBLE**, after all, is the great authority. It meets us just where conscience and reason fails us, and responds to and corroborates the profoundest and most indestructible intuitions of humanity.

Here the Bible comes forward and proclaims the fact of a coming judgment in the most emphatic and unmistakable language, and describes the principles on which are to follow from it, with the utmost minuteness. I have avoided quoting texts more than I could help in former lectures, mainly because the number corroborative of each of my points would have been so overwhelming; but I must necessarily quote three or four passages here, and shall take them from the words of Jesus, Paul, Peter, Jude, and John, that in the mouth of three or four witnesses this truth may be established.

"The hour is coming, in which all that are in the graves shall hear the voice of the Son of Man, and shall come forth; they that have done good, unto the resurrection of life; and they that have done evil, unto the resurrection of damnation" (John v. 28, 29).

"The Lord Jesus shall be revealed from heaven with His mighty angels, in flaming fire taking vengeance on them that know not God, and that obey not the gospel of our Lord Jesus Christ: who shall be punished with everlasting destruction from the presence of the Lord, and from the glory of His power" (2 Thess. i. 7-9).

"For we must all appear before the judgment seat of Christ; that every one may receive the things done in his body, according to that he hath done, whether it be good or bad" (2 Cor. v. 10).

"But the day of the Lord will come as a thief in the night; in the which the heavens shall pass with a great noise, and the elements shall melt with fervent heat, the earth also and the works that are therein shall be burnt up" (2 Peter iii. 10).

"And the angels which kept not their first estate, but left their own habitation, He hath reserved in everlasting chains under darkness unto the judgment of the great day" (Jude 6).

"And I saw a great white throne, and Him that sat on it, from whose face the earth and the heaven fled away; and there was found no place for them. And I saw the dead, small and great, stand before God; and the books were opened: and another book was opened, which is the book of life: and the dead were judged out of those things which were written in the books, according to their works" (Rev. xx. 11, 12).

I accept that authority. That answers to the voice of my conscience. That satisfies the claims of my intellect. Here I perceive that God will avenge the wrongs, not only of His own elect, but of the fatherless, the widow, and the oppressed of all ages, and the cry of my soul for justice is met, my sense of outraged righteousness is appeased, my conscience pronounces, "True and righteous art Thou, O King of saints!"

But people say, and a great many Christian people say in this day, "A good deal of the language in these and similar texts is figurative language." They do not like the doctrine; it is too definite, too particular, too inclusive for them; and so they try to explain it away. But supposing that some of the language were figurative,--what then? What do you gain by making it out to be figurative? What are figures for? Surely no one will argue that the judgment, as pre-figured in the words of Jesus Christ and His apostles, will be less thorough, less scrutinising, less terrible than the figures used to set it forth! Therefore it does not matter whether these be figurative expressions or no, seeing that they are calculated to convey the most awful and tremendous ideas of the judgment which any figures could convey, which the wisdom of God could select.

Some of the objections which people bring against the literal fulfilment of these passages seem to me to be very weak.

They say, "Where could be the scene of such a judgment seat?" I answer, He who created the universe can surely make a platform big enough on which to judge the inhabitants of this little world. For aught we know, there may be one already erected. There may be a world of judgment going on, where the representatives of the Divine government are already at work, getting ready for the final sentence. We do not know.

Again, they say, "Look at the time it would require." But I say, He who has had patience to watch the long procession of man's iniquities through the ages of time will perhaps have patience to judge men on account of them! And as one day is with the Lord as a thousand years, be sure, sinner, He will take the time to investigate your case; you will not be missed out.

Note that this judgment is to be **universal**.

These passages and numberless others declare that the dead, small and great, shall stand before God, and that **every** knee shall bow before Him, and **every** tongue confess to Him. If God in some way will deal individually with every son and every daughter of Adam, what does it signify where or by what method He does it, so that the end be secured? You and I will find our way from the spot, wherever it may be, to heaven or to hell, according to the sentence. Our destiny in the great eternity which follows will be settled by the **sentence**, not the method by which it is arrived at. The great matter to us is that "we must **all** appear before the judgment seat of Christ, that **every one** may receive the things done in his body, according to that he hath done, whether it be good or bad." This is not the Old Testament. I have purposely confined my quotations to the New; this is the revelation of the **gospel of Jesus Christ**, by which Paul declares God will "judge the secrets of men."

Not only will every man and woman be dealt with, but every character will be **demonstrated, made manifest**.

There will be no whited sepulchre business there, no make-believe sentimental salvation, no false gospel, with its creeds and phrases, no ceremonial salvation, but we shall all stand revealed as we are, black or white, good or bad, washed or unwashed, pure or impure.

What nonsense it is for people to talk of going down to death with their hearts full of iniquity,--"as a cage of unclean birds" as some of them are so fond of quoting. If so, what effect will death have upon their moral nature? What cleansing stream will be opened by the Angel of Death? If you are not saved from sin before you come down to the Jordan of death, there is no virtue in its waters to wash you. There is only one cleansing medium for **SOULS**, and that is the blood of the Lamb; and you must get washed in **life**, if you want to pass muster at death and at the judgment seat.

People say, "Do you think the sins of the saints are going to be dragged out at the judgment seat?" No! not the sins of the saints, for they are cast behind his back; but the saints themselves are going to be dragged out. One great end of the judgment will be to decide **who are the saints**, and to show to the universe that Jesus was equal to the work He had undertaken, namely, to destroy in the hearts of His saints the works of the devil, and that He was strong enough to hold them up against all the temptations and allurements of sin, blameless unto that day; and now they are to be revealed and held up, not as dark, hollow, evil-hearted, hypocritical people, but as the saints of God, washed and saved and made clean and white, which you know means holy, in the blood of the Lamb. He will point all the devils in the universe to His saints; they will be His boast and glory, and manifest victory over the devil. The question of questions then will be, Are you a saint?

Further, every character is not only to be settled and demonstrated, but it is to be **judged according to its deserts**-- "according to that he **hath done**."

He that knew his Master's will and did it not, is to be beaten with many stripes; while he who knew it not and did things worthy of stripes, is to be beaten with few. "And thou, Capernaum, which art exalted unto heaven, shalt be brought down to hell."

We shall be judged according to our privileges, according to the light we have received, and the obedience we have rendered to it, not only outwardly, but inwardly; according to our rebellion or submission to God; according to our loyalty and obedience to Him, in our hearts as well as in our lives.

I am afraid many, even of those who are saved, will suffer great loss in that day. There will be a great deal of wood, hay, and stubble, instead of gold, silver, and precious stones. Oh, let us wake up in time to redeem the few remaining days of our lives. The past is irredeemable; it is gone, and its losses must remain for ever. The harvest which we **might** have gathered is lost, and God Himself cannot make up to us for **that** loss. We may have many to-morrows, but we shall never have over again a yesterday. Oh! friends, you who love Him will have to stand before His judgment seat to receive the things **done** in the body. What are you doing? Are you visiting His sick or in prison? Are you ministering unto Him when hungry or naked, in the persons of His poor? When He is cast out and traduced in the persons of His persecuted ones, are showing your love to Him by standing up for His character and doing what you can to defend Him? Are you seeking after His lost sheep **diligently** until you find them, which means, you know, going after them **where they are**, however the thorns may prick your feet or the sun light on your head? Are you **DOING** these things? because, if not, don't expect Him to say, "Inasmuch as ye did it unto one of the least of these My brethren, ye have done it unto Me."

Can anybody imagine that Jesus Christ will pronounce a sort of figurative or sentimental judgment--that He will say, "Inasmuch as ye

~ Popular Christianity ~

did this or that" to those who never did anything of the kind? Such a proceeding would be very unlike anything He ever did or said when on earth, would it not? He was so true that He was called "**the Truth**;" so intensely real and practical that no shadow of unreality or sham could endure His gaze for a moment. Is it possible to conceive that He will be any other when He comes to judgment? And yet how many of His professed followers are presuming on a Judge all meekness, mercy, and love, quite forgetting that in that day the reign of mercy will be ended and the Lamb that was slain will appear as the Lion of the tribe of Judah, the Judge of all the earth, who will still **do right**.

What are you doing, friend? As the stories come to me from Hackney Wick, Seven Dials, St. Giles', the Borough, and other parts where our people are visiting and working continually,--stories of destitution, sickness, sorrow, and suffering, no less than of sin and crime and shame,--I feel, what can I do, what can I say that will arouse God's professed people to some concern and care for these poor lost multitudes? Our people tell me they find people who say "Don't talk to us about a God: we don't believe in such a Being. Don't tell us about Christians: we want neither you nor your tracts, nor your Bibles--away with you. We don't believe in such Christians, who leave us to die in want and misery like this." Men and women nearly naked, children absolutely so, women who must not look off from their match-box making, at 2½*d.* per gross, or their shirt stitching, at 3*d.* each, for fear of reducing their earnings a half-penny, and thus robbing their children of an ounce more bread, or the rent of their wretched room of the last fraction which an inexorable (perhaps Christian?) Landlord exacts. Thousands of such wretched beings, without a bed to lie upon, without fire to warm them, or sufficient food to keep body and soul together, are living in the greatest degradation and sin all over this London, perhaps not two hundred yards from the very spot where we are assembled this afternoon; and yet who cares for them, or visits them, or weeps over them with a really Christ-like sympathy? Who carried them either the bread that perisheth or the Bread of Life? You London Christians, what shall you say in the great day of account? Where shall you stand? How will you look? Oh, friends, give up the sentimental hypocrisy of singing,-- "Rescue the perishing, Care for the dying,"-- in the drawing-room to the accompaniment of the piano, without ever dreaming of going outside to do it; such idle words will prove only a mockery and a sham in the great day of account. Such songs will come booming back on the ears of the soul with more awful forebodings that the echoes of the Archangel's trumpet itself! Sentimentalism will have no resurrection; it will rot with the grave clothes! What doth it profit, my brethren, to say to the hungry and naked, either physically or spiritually, Be ye warmed and filled, if, notwithstanding, ye give them not either the temporal or the spiritual bread? He will say, "Inasmuch as ye did **it not**, depart from Me."

Further, the verdict of that day will carry universal conviction.

Every being will feel that long-waited-for justice has come at last. The song which will burst forth from the lips of the saints, as they take their places in the celestial city, will be, "True and righteous art Thou, O King of saints;" and methinks the same words, though not uttered by the lips, will be graven on the hearts of the hosts of the lost as they sink to meet their doom, and the realization of the justice of their sentence will make their hell. May no soul in this assembly, nor any who may read these words, ever realize what this means. Amen.

NOTES OF THREE ADDRESSES ON HOUSEHOLD GODS

DELIVERED IN STEINWAY HALL, REGENT STREET

"Know ye not, that to whom ye yield yourselves servants to obey, his servants ye are to whom ye obey; whether of sin unto death, or of obedience unto righteousness?" --*Romans vi. 16.*

IT is assumed all through this Book that every human being has a deity. In fact, we are so made that we must have a God. Even the man who says there is no God, worships a god notwithstanding, and that god is, "to whom he yields himself a servant to obey." Now God claims to be the Deity of the soul of every human being; but Satan has supplanted God, and he has done it in many ways. He has assumed many different forms in order to suit different classes and conditions of men. For one class of person he finds one idol, for another class another. But the principle laid down is, that whatever the outward form may be, that which usurps in a man's affections, life, and action, **the place of God**, becomes his deity. He need not outwardly label it **idol**, or bow his knees and worship it. The supremacy which he gives to it in his affections and life is the point.

What an awful thought that in this so-called Christian England, tens of thousands of people are as truly worshipping idols as are any of the inhabitants of Africa or China.

I want this morning to confine myself more particularly to the gods of the household. Professing Christians speak about giving up the vanities of the world, and coming out from the world, when, alas! we need not go outside the four walls of their own dwellings to find their god. I am afraid there are quite as many people who go wrong with these inside idols as with the outside ones.

The first that strikes us as the most universal god of so-called religious society in this day is the

God of Fashion

Now, what is fashion? What does the term mean? It means the world's way of having things, and the world's way of doing things.

When we look abroad on the great majority of men and women around us, we see that they are utterly godless, selfish, and untrue, and yet the majority always fixes the fashion. It is not the few true, real, God-fearing, earnest men and women who want to serve God and help humanity who fix the fashion; it is always the majority. Consequently, you see fashion is always diametrically opposed to God's way of having things, and God's way of doing things. Therefore, the votaries of fashion cannot possibly be the servants of God! There is no getting away from that conclusion.

Let us now inquire what is God's great **end** or purpose in His way of doing things, and in the way that He has prescribed in which we are to have and to do things. What is shown by the constitution of our bodies, by the laws and ordinances of the heaven, and by the laws of nature, to be God's end in everything? Utility! If you look at your eye, or study your ear or hands, or any other part of your body, you cannot find a single fibre or nerve which is not of some use in your animal economy--nothing superfluous, nothing for waste or for the mere sake of being there. A useful result is the end contemplated. Look at the heavens--it is the same; there is not a single waste star. Look at the animal creation--it is the same. Look at the vegetable creation--it is the same. The very rocks exist not for themselves. The earth ministers to the wants of man and beast. There is nothing created for mere show, no useless part of creation. The aim of God in all His modes and works is the highest food to all His creatures. Now let us inquire what is the **end** of fashion. When we substitute the means for the end, we lose the great result God has in store for us. This is true in everything, natural, mental, and spiritual. Now, God's order is to have everything attuned to the highest result, especially in the case of His highest creature--man. He wants us to use ever power and capacity He has given us for the highest ends--to serve God and humanity! But fashion has turned God's order topsy-turvy, and set up as its end, supposed Beauty! **not** that beauty which is an accomplishment of utility; but fashion sets up beauty as the **end**, and not the accompaniment. Fashion says, "That is elegant. That looks grand, so it shall be so." So the great question comes to be in dress, in equipage, in our modes of doing business, in our furnishing arrangements, and in our institutions, What is the order of fashion? Fashion sets the law, and everybody does what everybody else does; and all who will not bow down to this idol are called puritans, fanatics, straight-laced, or by any other terms of contempt

~ Popular Christianity ~

most convenient. So hot is this furnace of contempt and scorn that it is one of the highest tests of moral courage in man or woman to set fashion at naught. It is one of the grandest things to teach your children from their babyhood to say, "No, I won't do that because everybody else does it. You must give me a better reason than the fashion for what I do."

Fashion prescribes the form of dress for almost the whole world. Doctors may talk, and advise, and warn against high heels, tight waists, and insufficient clothing, and all the monstrous and ridiculous appendages to dress which fashion from time to time prescribes. But it is fashion! that is enough. Never mind if tight-lacing does squeeze my lungs and prevent me from getting the necessary amount of air, thus inducing premature disease or death; it is the fashion, and I must do it. Never mind if the high-heeled shoes produce deformity of the spine and all manner of other injuries; it is the fashion, and I must have them. I must dress myself in the most ridiculous costumes which Parisian milliners can contrive, it is the fashion; if the dress is too light, or does not half cover my body, never mind; I shall wear it because it is the fashion.

So, in the furnishing of people's houses, in a great many instances, it is the same. I have been in many houses where it seems to me that almost all utility and necessary comfort for health and work is lost sight of. It is almost all show, so that you are afraid to use a table for fear you will injure it. Oh, the money and time that are squandered, and the perpetual strife that goes on to keep up this show because everybody else does it.

In their very companionships fashion has decided what should be the ground and the rule of selection, and so fashionable people have only the companions that society has settled they **are to have**. They do not look, as you would suppose rational beings would, for congenial society in the way of congeniality of thought, and feeling, and intelligence, that which gives vivacity and interest to communion with another. Oh, no! If a person ever so attractive and clever, and competent to interest, or instruct, or please them, happens to be a grade lower on the social scale, fashion says, "That person is not in your circle, he is out of your sphere; you cannot associate with such a person." So they deprive their intellects and hearts of the greatest delight, because fashion has prescribed what kind of people they

~ *Catherine Booth* ~

should associate with, and if those people be ever so hollow and empty, never mind; they must obey the behests of **fashion**.

Fashion has also settled that it is not the thing for people in certain positions and stations to go to such and such **places**, but that it is right for them to go to others, and so they go wherever fashion dictates. Fashion has even prescribed the way people shall move and the way in which they shall speak, and has got them pretty much squozen down into uniformity, so that all naturalness is lost and they are nearly all alike. It is the same kind of movement they make and the same kind of platitudes they utter, everywhere and in all circumstances. I hope there are not many of this class here this morning; but if there are any, let me ask, How do you like the picture-- the representation of the claims of this Deity?--that rational beings, intelligent creatures, some of them capable of great and glorious things, should be thus fettered and bound and squozen into one shape and reduced to nonentities and puppets?

Do you envy the fate of the devotees of fashion? Will **you** worship this god any longer? Thank God, He emancipated me twenty-five years ago, and I have been free ever since. If you are not yet emancipated, get emancipated this morning.

Do not consider fashion when you are settling how you ought to order your household, but plan for the highest good of your children and those around you, and for your greatest usefulness in the world. Never mind fashion.

In this day when chaplains of prisons and reformatories tell us that gaudy, flashy dressing leads as many young girls to destruction as drink, it behoves every true woman to settle before God in her closet what kind of dress she ought to wear, and to resolve to wear it in spite of fashion. If all professedly Christian ladies would do this, what a salvation this one reform alone would work in the world! You young people here resolve that you will be original natural human beings, as God would have you; resolve that you won't be squozen into this mould, or into that, to please anybody--that you will be an independent man or woman, educated and refined by intercourse with God; but **be yourself**, and do not aim to be anybody else. Set fashion at nought. If people would do this, what different households they would have! What different children! What different friends! What different results they would produce in the world, and how differently they would feel when they were dying! Oh, what wasted lives! What beautiful forms,

~ Popular Christianity ~

and beautiful minds, and beautiful intellects are prostrated and ruined at the shrine of the god of fashion! May God deliver us from this idol!

Another of the most prominent of household gods is that of ease--comfort. In may instances the highest interests of the children and servants, the good of the bodies and souls of men, the serving and glory of God, are all made subservient to this god of comfort.

Think for a moment what God requires of every human being. First, He requires all men to be His people; and secondly, He requires of all His people that they should be absolutely **HIS SERVANTS**.

Now then, compare the duties of a servant with the idea of ease and comfort being the prevailing notion of a man's life, and you will see its absurdity. What would you think of a servant, whose prevailing idea was to make her or himself **comfortable**? Suppose such a one saying, "Yes, I want the situation, I should like the wages, but I want my comfort most. I do not want to get up any earlier in the morning than the mistress or the master. I am not going to do any hard or troublesome work. I don't see why I should. I should like an easy chair to sit in, and certain hours of the day to myself. I am not going to do this or the other that is disagreeable to me. I am going to be **COMFORTABLE**." What would you think of such a servant?

You smile; well, if we are true and real, we have given up the ownership of ourselves. We have become literally the slaves of the living God, to do His bidding, to work for His interests, to look after His lost ones, to extend His kingdom, and to live for His glory! **This** is what we **PROFESS**. This is not The Salvation Army theology only. This is in all Church creeds, more or less. It was sworn over your baptismal font that you should renounce the devil and all his works, that you should give up "the world" and be a true and real servant of the Most High God. And yet I am afraid many in this congregation have taken good care never to serve God at the expense of their own **comfort**! If you suggest any plan of usefulness, the first thing that meets you in one form or another is, "Oh, that would be hard work; that would be a sacrifice; or, I should have to give up so many evenings a week;" or sometimes, alas, "that would interfere with my dinner hour."

These ease-loving Christians do not look at the object that has to be accomplished for God; but how it will effect their own ease and comfort. "I visit the poor! Oh, I could not; think of the smells I should have to encounter; look at the disagreeable sights I should have to see!

~ *Catherine Booth* ~

My delicate nerves would not bear it. Oh, no, I could not. If the Lord has any nice comfortable work, I have no objection; but my comfort must first be considered. Your mission services are all very good, but we cannot have our household duties upset. We must have our domestic regularity--our comfort." I have wept many a times as I have parted with such people, when these words forced themselves upon me: "Saul returned into his own house, but David gat him into the hold."

David must go and fight and face the perils of the wilderness, and endure all sorts of self-sacrifice, and conflict, and sorrow, but Saul goes back to his own house. He has done with it. He thinks his responsibility is at an end. When the meeting is over, these people who have heard all about the claims of God and the lost, and perhaps said a few sleepy words of sympathy, or given a five-pound note, away they go to their own houses; but the real Davids must get up into the holds, or else God's armies will be wasted, and hell will be more largely people that it would be otherwise. Somebody must hold the fort, somebody must fight, somebody must suffer. Nothing can be done for humanity but through suffering, and if one won't, there falls a double weight upon another. Oh, the multitudes of souls who have made shipwreck through this god of ease! It ruins the soul that worships, as well as hinders all the good that might be done for others. It has a stupefying, paralysing, damning influence upon every soul that once gives way to it.

Once get under the domination of **THAT GOD**, and you are done for. If you are under his domination, for Christ's sake get up this morning and ask Him to snap the fetters that bind you. Jesus from the Cross cries to you. Suffering humanity is sinking at this hour by thousands into a hell on earth, and a nethermost hell hereafter. Up, Christians, arise and be doing! Put off your sleepiness, your idleness, and set to work; bend **your** back to the burden, stoop to pick up the lost. They are crying all around you for help.

If I understand this book, you will be called to an awful account if your opportunity, your strength of body, your capacities for blessing your fellow-men are all buried and destroyed by this love of ease.

Thank God, He emancipated me from that years ago. I have had the same temptations that others have had, and perhaps sometimes even extra temptations, through excessive weariness, frequently hardly knowing how to get from my bed; but I have had such a horror of

~ Popular Christianity ~

getting under the dominion of this god of ease that I have set my whole nature against it.

What would you think of a mother whose child was dangerously sick saying, "Really, I am so burdened with the rest of my family, I have so much to think about, that I cannot give myself up to this child. I am very sorry, of course, I feel it very deeply, but I cannot deny myself of the comforts of life. I must lie on the sofa so long, and I must do this, that, or the other, or go here and there?" What would you think of such a woman? And yet there are thousands of professing Christians who lie on the sofa, I am afraid, half their time. They don't know what to do with themselves, trying to get amused and occupied, and yet they profess to be God Almighty's **SERVANTS!**

My friends, put this practical test to yourselves. It is of no use going to services and hearing beautiful sermons which you don't apply to yourselves. Are not these things realities? If so, I say, for Christ's sake, for your soul's sake, and humanity's sake, act accordingly.

Another household god--alas! I wish it could be kept out of the household (for it is more especially the god of the world outside, yet it comes into the family and gets into the hearts of the very little ones)--

The God of Gain

Now God's order is for every man to look after his fellow man-- "look not every man on his own things, but also on the things of others," but the world's order--its received maxim is--"every man for himself." God's order is, "As ye would men should do to you, do ye even so to them." That means, you know, when you are making a bargain, don't run a man down below the lawful price of his goods, any more than you would like him to run you down. Don't beat down that poor woman in her work because you know she has no one to appeal to. That is the spirit of selfishness, which is of the devil.

This god of gain, how I see its sway sometimes in houses where I stay. What a contrast I often see between the interest excited by the news of the day, and any information respecting the kingdom of God. You know how morning prayers are got over very often--how superficial it all is, how little heart there is in it. It seems quite a relief to the worshippers when it is over; then begins the real interest of the day. The gentleman seizes the newspaper, looks up and down the columns to see how the funds stand. If you keep looking at him you will tell in a minute if there is anything in the paper that touches him. If he is a merchant, the state of the market as to the things he buys or sells touches him to the quick; if he sees something affecting his interests he will perhaps tell it to the wife, and then you will see the older children looking towards him with the greatest anxiety--the god of gain has his hand even on their young hearts. They may have some outward show of being religious, but gain is the real god. If there is anything that entails immediate action in connection with the business, you see how everything else is at once put on one side. Then the lady says, "business must be attended to." **Must** is a *sine qua non* in the matter. Would to God they would put a **must** in somewhere else. The children all know the importance of that must. They know, perhaps, that they have money, that they are to be rich some day, but nevertheless they want more. Their father cannot afford to lose if he has ever so much. Gain, gain--they must make gain! That man may see in another column of the paper something which affects the work of God, but he only says a few sleepy words about it, "very sorry, very sorry indeed." Then down goes the paper, and he gets ready to go to his office. The column touching his gains touched him to the quick, the other only touched his sentimentality; the one touched **his** interests, the other touched only those of Jesus Christ.

Once I was at a conference, and I shall never forget it. I saw a company of ministers deliberating on certain questions, and the questions were all on paper, so that everybody knew what was coming on. I noticed that when anything came up affecting the character, or position, or income of those individuals, every man was in his place, every man had his papers and pencil, quick as lightning, to catch every word that was said. But when it was a question that only referred to the work of God, to the interests of the Church, to the salvation of souls, a number of them were out of their places altogether. Others had got the newspapers, others were writing letters. There was only a handful who were paying proper attention to the question. I thought, O my God, it is as it was in the days of old, "there is not one of them that will keep Thy doors for nought; they are all gone after their covetousness." Don't call that censorious. You know how true it is. I **WISH IT WERE NOT**. I feel as if I could give the blood out of my very heart that it might not be so, **but it is so**. I have no doubt the Apostle was forced much against his will to say and feel--"For all seek their own, not the things which are Jesus Christ's." Alas! it had begun to be true then;

~ Popular Christianity ~

how much more true is it now? I trust and believe that God is raising up a people who will seek His, in their very hearts' core, and who will be willing to sacrifice their own gain!

"The love of money is the root of all evil." Human experience justifies the Divine word. Show me a man who loves money for its own sake, for the sake of hoarding it and leaving it to his children, and I will show you a man whom the **THE DEVIL IS SURE OF**. There is no doubt about it, unless God in His omnipotent mercy awakens him and gives him grace to turn that devil of avarice out of his soul--"Covetousness, which is idolatry"--idol worship! gold worship! wealth worship!!

Are you worshipping this god? My friend, make haste for your life. You can no more be the Lord's servant and worship wealth, than the Jews were who crucified the Lord Jesus.

Friends, go to your closets; see whether you are in any measure under the domination of this idol of gain! see why you value your money; see what you purpose to do with it; reckon, if you had a husband, a wife, or

child in slavery, and you could buy them out, how much of the money you would keep. Reckon what you ought to keep while thousands of your brethren are the slaves of sin and the devil, when your money would help to deliver them. Reckon this matter as you would reckon with your steward.

You give your steward possession of certain property to manage for you; you know that he must eat and drink, and have a place to rest in; if he is a good servant, you say, "Here, John, I want you to accomplish that work for me in so many months, and I place at your disposal these resources. Get in these debts, see these creditors, receive such and such moneys, do such and such things. You may take out all that is necessary to keep you in comfort and in health (and if he has a family), as much as your family requires, not for extravagance, but for your necessary comfort, while you are doing my business." Would you reckon that such a steward had a right to spend your money in extravagant living, or hoard it up for his own personal ends? Are you a steward of God? And do you expect to give an account to Him who shall judge both quick and dead? If so, what will you say when He demands an account of your stewardship?

The household god next in importance, and which is perhaps the most popular both of the household and the nation, is the

God of Education

Everything must bow to the scholastic education of the children. Their very health is sacrificed in hundreds of instances; the whole of the domestic arrangements, the convenience of father and mother and visitors must bow down to this god. The children must be educated, whatever else becomes of them. I touched very briefly on this subject in my address at Exeter Hall on "Family Religion," and some friends seemed to infer that I was against education, whereas I have seldom talked with any one on the subject more profoundly impressed with its importance! I adopted, many years ago, the sentiment of the philosopher Locke, who said that "in nine cases out of ten all the men we meet are what they are for good or for evil, for usefulness or otherwise, by their education." I say I fully believe that, and have acted upon it in training my own family; so you see my quarrel is not with education, but with a certain **kind** of education.

I believe that a child ought to be educated every half-hour of its life--never ought to be left to itself in the sense of not having a recognised influence exerted over its mind. The question is then, What **kind** of education is the right kind to bestow upon children? How ought you to educate them? The same idea which helped us on the question of fashion my help us again here. What should be the great purpose of education? Surely right education must be that which is calculated to help the child to attain the **highest type of its kind**, and to fit it for its highest destiny. You train your horse on that principle. You develop and strengthen it that it may be a perfect creature, having capacity developed for the highest service of which its nature is capable. I say that all right training ought to contemplate this end, and especially with respect to man, God's highest creature. Next comes the question, What **is** the highest type of a man? and the highest destiny of a man? What ought we to aim at? For if the aim is wrong, all our training will be wrong. I say that the highest type of a man is that in which the **soul** rules over the body, in which a purified, ennobled soul rules through an enlightened intelligence, and makes every faculty of the being subservient to the highest purpose, the service of humanity and the service of God! If I understand it, that is the highest type of man and his highest destiny. And it seems to me that all education that falls short of this is a curse rather than a blessing.

The aim of all rightly directed education is to make such men and women, and to fit them for such work, and if it fails of this, I say it is one-sided, unphilosophical, and irreligious, and **THAT IS MY QUARREL WITH MODERN EDUCATION**. I charge it with being all this, and that is the reason I did not educate my children after its theories; I did not believe in them, and the results so far prove that I was right.

Then first let me look at what ought to be the purpose of education. Most of you, nearly all, I presume, agree as to what I have stated. But the purpose of modern education is anything but this. It is for the most part planned and executed with a view to the aggrandisement or well-being of the individual, looked at in a worldly point of view. Parents look at their boy and say, "Now, what can we do with him?" They have all sorts of aspirations and ambitions for the boy, and they say, "Well, we must educate him, develop his intellect"-- what for? That he may use it for the service of humanity and the glory of God? Oh no, that never enters their minds. They say, "We will have him educated in order that he may shine in the world, or get up in the world. We will have a son who will be able to go to the bar, the senate house, or do anything else that their ambition fixes on. The **AGGRANDISEMENT OF THE INDIVIDUAL** is the end, not the universal good, and out of this wrong aim arises the undue estimate of mere scholastic education. What would you say of the training of an animal, if it were possible for the trainer to select one or two faculties, and develop and strengthen them to the exclusion, neglect, or extinction of other faculties? Would you say that was right training?

The main idea of modern education is that of the imparting of knowledge. Knowledge is the idol which both the household and the nation to-day are worshipping more largely perhaps than any other, as if progress in knowledge constituted the true progress of man. Oh, if it were so, what a different world we should have to-day; but we know it is quite the contrary. We know that the more knowledge you give to an individual, without giving him a corresponding disposition to use it for good, the more you increase his capacity for mischief. Very often the most learned men live for the worst purposes! But, alas! the very flower of the youth of our nation are sacrificed to this modern deity. The notion is that our youth must be educated in this mischievous sense; they must be crammed with knowledge; whether it be a curse or a blessing to them is not the question, **but they must have it**. They must learn the dead languages, and read bad literature, in order to make them like the rest of the world around them, no matter what becomes of their morals; they must be crammed with science,--much of it falsely so called; much of it in embryo, crude and shallow--the shallow theories of minds trying to grasp profound thoughts, and getting lost in the fogs of their own folly, landing the poor pupils on the strand of infidelity and atheism. The intellect, the one faculty of the man, must be strained, and stretched, and crammed to the utter neglect, and often destruction, of the moral faculties. And when you have done, what have you produced? An enlightened animal, an intellectual monster, who walks abroad, treading under his feet all the tender instincts and most sacred feelings and aspirations of humanity. That is all you have produced; there are thousands such to be seen to-day. Alas! my heart bleeds over the stories I hear all over the land, which I could give you as illustrations of this fact. All this mischief comes of upsetting God's order--cultivating the intellect at the expense of the **heart**; being at more pains to make our youth **clever** than to make them **GOOD**!

This false theory leads to false methods, and hence the deplorable condition of our nation to-day. It leads to the separating from home life our little boys of ten and twelve years of age, and our little girls too, alas! sending them away from the tender influences, and what ought to be the grand and noble inspirations of their mothers, to herd with boys of their own age and class, to have their moral nature manipulated by masters, often sceptical or immoral. Now I say and will maintain that the chief end of education is not mere teaching, but **INSPIRATION**; and if you fail to inspire your pupil with nobleness, disinterested goodness, truth, morality, and religion, not only are all the glorious ends of education lost, but you damn your pupil more deeply than he might have been damned without your education. I ask, Is it not so? Take some of your own sons (alas! I could point to numbers round about) as illustrations of this fact. God has given every child a tutor in his mother, and she is the best and only right tutor for the heart.

I defy you to fill a proper mother's place for influence over the heart. If God were to depute the angel Gabriel, he could not do it. God has tied the child to its mother by such peculiar moral and mental links that no other being could possibly possess. I tell you mothers here, that if you are good mothers, you are committing the greatest wrong to send away your child from your homes, and I believe this wretched

~ Popular Christianity ~

practice is ruining half our nation to-day. God committed the child to its parents to be educated, not to the schoolmaster. You can employ the schoolmaster to teach his head,--and even then you must be very careful of what sort he is, or he will ruin the child; but God committed the child to the parents to be educated, trained--that is, taught how to **feel, think**, and **act**. And it is to the mother especially belongs the art and the capacity to inspire her boy to love all that is noble and good, and disinterested, and grand in humanity, and to keep on inspiring him until he is strong enough in God's likeness and grace to walk alone. Just as you tend him when he is a baby, and will not leave him to strangers, so, while he is a moral infant, you are to watch and keep and train him until he is able to walk alone. I set my soul on this with regard to my own children, and God has enabled me to do it. I had a great fight over it in many ways, but I said, "I am **determined** to keep my children for God and goodness. They shall have the education that I think likely to help them to be useful to their generation, as far as possible; but I will never sacrifice purity to polish, I will never sacrifice the heart to the head." That was my resolve, and I see no cause to regret it.

I think it was Fenelon who said that "the service of my family is more important than the service of myself, and the service of my nation is more important than the service of my family, and the service of my humanity is more important than the service of my nation." That is my opinion. This is God's idea of man's highest vocation: "The Son of Man is come to seek and to save that which was lost." If God's type of manhood had been a being crammed with knowledge to the exclusion of the moral and religious sentiments, Jesus Christ would have been such a man, whereas He was the opposite. He combined all the tenderness, sublime devotion, and self-sacrifice of the woman with the intellect and strength of a man. He was God's model man. That is the type for us. Therefore, for the sake of your children and your own grey hairs, I beseech you to see to it that you train and educate them in His likeness. Alas! I know many parents in this land to-day, who are wringing their hands in anguish for the consequences of a false notion of education, and yet there are tens of thousands more who are making the same experiment, to have the same results.

I was staying in a mansion some time ago, where there was everything that wealth and refinement could procure to make the parents happy. But I thought as I looked at the dear old gentleman--one of the kindly type of man, at whose table you like to sit down because of the genial intercourse and the generous sympathies of his soul towards all humanity--but I thought there seemed to be a gloom over the household. I felt as if he had a sorrowful spirit, though I knew not why. After dinner, when we got into the library, he said, with trembling lips,--

"I wish you could get a word with E--."

I said, "Who is that?"

"My eldest son; do try to get a minute to speak with him."

"Why, what is the matter?" I said.

"I am afraid he has embraced sceptical opinions, I sent him to a professedly Christian school (ah, I thought, the old story!) and then to college, and now I am afraid he is nearly an infidel."

And when I got hold of the young gentleman I saw that he was just of the type our modern schools produce--self-conceited, proud, vain; a young man who looked down on his father as much as an antiquated picture or piece of furniture. Oh, these stories, they break my heart! I felt that this dear old man spent his money on the education of his son, and thought he was doing the best he could for him, to send him to a so-called Christian school and then to a so-called Christian college, and here is the result; and there are thousands of such results!

Yet people send their sons over and over again to these schools and colleges, commit them knowingly to sceptical and infidel teachers--give them over, body, mind, and soul to them, to go through a process of education which necessitates the putting into their hands of text books containing all matter of idolatrous legends and impure and immoral histories, bringing into their imaginations all manner of profanities and impurities just at the most critical period of their history. And this is all done under the name of **"CHRISTIAN EDUCATION!"**

I could tell you stories that would make you weep almost tears of blood at the consequences of these associations. Don't I know mothers to-day who are wringing their hands in agony, and fathers who are bowed down almost to the grave, broken-hearted, because of them? Add to this education association with troops of godless, lawless, and frequently immoral youths, whom they are sure to have for their companions, and then wonder that youths isolated from their mothers, sisters, and all the refining and religious influences of home life--put into these schools and colleges, and kept there frequently for seven or eight years, and I ask, Can parents be surprised that they receive them back without any principles, without any love for their parents, without any religion, and without any respect for humanity? to walk about and trample under foot the most sacred instincts, and feelings, and aspirations of true manhood and womanhood, and to march over the nation to spread desolation and ruin wherever they go--moral waifs and strays--drifting down the current of humanity, down, down to everlasting shame?

This is the result of modern education falsely so called. I challenge anybody to disprove it. Now then I say, let ever Christian parent in his closet settle before God this matter. What will you make your child? Will you say, "I will be more concerned that he shall be a good, benevolent, holy man, working for the good of his race, than that he shall be one of those intellectual monsters, all head and no heart. I will rather that he should be poor and good than that he should be rich and wicked"? When you come to that, you will save your children. But you say, "Well, I must have this position and that position for him, not because of the use he will be to humanity and the glory he will bring to God, but because he will be a bigger man, having social position and influence." Ah! thousands have said that, and their sons have ended in being nobodys--idle, extravagant, spend-thrifts, taking all the patrimony of their brothers and sisters to keep them going in their evil courses. Truly, "God is not mocked: whatsoever a man soweth, that shall he also reap."

~ *Catherine Booth* ~

THE SALVATION ARMY FOLLOWING CHRIST

BY COMMISSIONER RAILTON

DURING the past twenty years there has been growing up in the midst of Christendom an organization which has been all along denounced and opposed, in a manner remarkably resembling the opposition shown to Christ and His apostles by the religious and respectable people of their day. The very phrases applied to the latter have been those most commonly used in connection with the Salvation Army.

Such expressions as "blasphemy," "blasphemous performance," "mockery of religion," have been repeatedly used by the most thoughtful and influential critics with respect to this organization, and for what reason? Simply because poor and unlettered men and women are found continually expressing an intimate acquaintance with God in terms almost identical with those which are common in the Psalms and the Gospels. The poor man cries, and the Lord hears and delivers him; the convicted publican smites on his breast and crys, "God be merciful to me a sinner," but the unbelieving onlooker denounce his crying as an "intolerable noise," and his declaration that he has been delivered, an "unwarrantable presumption." It is notorious that in thousands of buildings next Sunday, congregations of people who, a few years ago, had nothing whatever to do with the worship of God, will be repeating exactly such-like experiences. Yet even some of those who regard these people with a somewhat friendly eye will excuse their making "a joyful noise unto the Lord" as a "pardonable extravagance," and will explain that it is due to their "want of culture" that they do not worship God in the "decorous silence" which is customary in modern places of worship. As for the greater part of the community, they will denounce the whole of the proceedings as an "outrageous nuisance," "a farce," etc., which "ought to be put down," or got rid of, if it were possible, and which it is to be hoped "will not last long."

Now it is a remarkable fact, worthy of the most careful study by all who would understand either the power of God or the times in which we live, that in the face of all this hostile opposition this Army

~ Popular Christianity ~

will go on without altering its course in the slightest degree to gain public favour, and that in fact it has gone on steadily increasing during twenty years, in spite of such opposition.

Ffive years ago this Army had only 442 corps and 1,067 officers--persons, that is to say, employed in the work and supported by it. During the year 1882 no less than 669 of the soldiers,--251 of them women--were knocked down, kicked, or brutally assaulted in the streets; fifty-six of the 530 buildings used were attacked and partially wrecked, and eighty-six officers or soldiers, fifteen of them women, were locked up and imprisoned by the authorities in connection with the open-air services. Bishops, editors of religious papers, chairmen of great religious assemblies united to denounce the Army in the extremest terms; but at the end of five years it is found to consist of 2,153 corps, under the leadership of more than 5,200 officers.

Now, if it be correct that the Army systematises blasphemy, this prodigious increase is truly a calamity; but if, on the contrary, it is found that thousands whose every second sentence was formerly an oath, and who neither feared God nor regarded man, are now to be seen clothed and in their right minds, singing (though it may be in rough style) the praises of God and living honest, industrious, and benevolent lives; then surely these figures eloquently demonstrate that the truth lies entirely on the other side, and that this vast working-class organizations is, after all, acting in conformity with the will of God, and therefore blessed and helped by Him, involving the inevitable conclusion that the common opinion of the day is in violent opposition to the spirit and work of Jesus of Nazareth.

Let us examine a little more closely the methods of the Army's increase, as illustrated by one of its most recent advances. A couple of young girls, formerly engaged in domestic service, declare themselves to be called to go out and preach the Gospel. For this purpose they place themselves at the disposal of the only religious organization in the world which thinks it right to give them this opportunity, and after careful examination into their character, they are sent off to a foreign country, where they are to raise an Army corps in a certain small town. The building in which they are to gather in their congregation is simply a long-disused workshop, where a number of unbacked seats have been placed. There is not a single person in the town who can be regarded as friendly to their mission, and most people consider their appointment as directly opposed to the will of Christ. Yet night after night their humble barracks are crowded with an audience consisting mainly of persons who have never worshipped God before. The meetings are interrupted, and violent scenes sometimes occur. Yet, as is common all over the world, those two officers have raised a corps in a short time.

And what is their corps? It consists of working men and women who are ready to stand up in the meetings and add their testimony to that of their officers, that Jesus Christ is a living Saviour. In the language of apostles and psalmists, not quoted but reproduced almost in identical terms from their own experience, they say that they were up to the time of their coming to these meetings "afar off by sin and wicked words, but have now been brought nigh to God by the blood of the Cross;" that He has filled their hearts with peace and gladness such as they never found while in pursuit of worldly pleasure,--a peace and gladness which rather increase than diminish under the scorn and opposition of family, friends, and workmates. It is not long before some of these converts are found expressing their highest ideal of duty in the desire to do exactly what their officers did when they left home, situation, worldly comforts and prospects, and embarked on a life of poverty and difficulty such as they have seen worked out before their eyes, in order to spread the glad tidings of a real Saviour from sin, whom they personally know.

Every step in the Army's progress has been accomplished in some such way as this, and the astonishment to most of us is not that such results should follow, but that people of intelligence should either continue with their eyes closed to it all, as though it had no existence, or else with persistence object, as though the Army were violating in every way the will of God, Again I say, this drives one inevitably to one of two conclusions,--either the army must be a system of the most terribly God-dishonouring delusion,--a curse to the world of the most awful kind, or else, if it be indeed what it professes to be, inspired, moved, and directed by Him--then the peoples of our day must have departed far from the spirit and teaching of God, both by His prophets and His Son, to have come into direct collision with these forces acting under His leadership.

If we search still more deeply into the secret of the Army's life and activities we shall find at every step the phenomen of a faith and practice exactly similar to those which the language of psalmists and apostles, literally taken, describe. Here are poor fishermen, who declare that they have heard Jesus Christ calling them to leave all and follow Him. They say that He walks by their side on the shore and sails with them over the stormy deep; that they commune with Him in the night watches; that whereas, but a short time ago, they were so utterly in darkness as to know nothing of the possibility of prayer, they now see clearly those great spiritual truths which have sustained their comrades in ages past; that God Himself is their light, and gives them to see, day by day, amidst the most toilsome occupations and the most ruffianly surroundings, more and more of Himself and His will concerning them. Nobody pretends to question that the lives of multitudes of such men have been, as the result of their connection with this Army, transformed as completely as they themselves declare that their inward experiences have been. Here are people who, but a few years ago, received with blows and curses those who spoke to them in the name of Christ, but who now manifest the same tender love towards those who ill-treat as was shown in the first place towards themselves--men and women who gladly bear contempt, abuse, poverty, and suffering of every kind, that they may spend the part of life which still remains to them in proclaiming their Saviour; men and women whose want of education and of many qualifications that one would suppose to be desirable for such a work, cannot prevent from profoundly impressing the souls, and thus changing the lives of multitudes of others. How is it all to be accounted for? We must either accept their own account of the marvel, and conclude that it is by the power of Jesus of Nazareth that these men see and walk thus in the presence of us all, or else we must find some other way of accounting for the change wrought in them.

Attempts of this kind have indeed been made, but they do not commend themselves to very serious attention. "Excitement--all excitement!" some have said. But has religious excitement ever been known to last for years consecutively in individual cases? Generally speaking, the duration of a wave of popular excitement upon any subject is to be measured by weeks, or by months at most. But here we have huge audiences gathered continuously, Sunday after Sunday,
for years, and men and women devoting themselves to the holding of services said to be of the "most exhausting character," night after night, without intermission. How can any mere excitement account for all this?

A somewhat more reasonable theory is that the Army owes all its successes to a "rigid discipline." But is not this begging the whole question? That the Army maintains and extends its influence largely as the result of military order and system is undoubtedly true; but the question is how men and women, hitherto averse to all religious control, and indeed, control of any kind, are induced to submit themselves without fee or reward to the orders of those who are often in every way their inferiors. Look at that young lad, not out of his teens, commanding a corps in some large city. His every sign is obeyed by men and women old enough to be his grandparents, by tradesmen who were accustomed to manage business affairs before he learned arithmetic (what little he knows of it), by sergeants and soldiers of the Army, who have served years longer than himself in it, and some of whom know more of God and mankind, more of the work and literature of the Army, than he does. Whence all this ready obedience, this systematic labour under such leadership? It is easy to explain all upon "the love of Christ constraineth us" principle, "submitting yourselves one to another in love;" but take that away, and what becomes of the Army"s discipline?

The Army's discipline is all the more remarkable when we remember that it is applied amongst all nations alike, and that in the world's three greatest Republics it is carried out as successfully as amongst communities more accustomed to the idea of submission to absolute authority. Moreover, the marvel of general and absolute obedience, rendered without murmuring by persons of all sorts and conditions, scattered all over the world, is all the more striking at a time when any approach to the exercise of authority in connection with religious work is becoming more and more out of the question.

Just consider for a moment what this Army discipline amounts to. Forty thousand times this week, and **every** week of this hot summer, bodies of men and women are induced, after having toiled all day at their usual employment, to walk more or less considerable distance from their homes, and place themselves under the leadership of officers who keep them from two to three hours engaged in praying, singing, speaking, marching through the streets, standing in narrow dirty alleys and courts, or sitting on unbacked seats in the close atmosphere of uncomfortable buildings. Yet this only represents the public services of the Army. We give up in despair any attempt to calculate the number of hours spent by scores of thousands of these soldiers in visiting, *War Cry* selling, and other labours, under the direction of their officers. All this will bear investigation and consideration to any extent; and the more it is considered, the more inevitable will be the conclusion that the Army's strength within and without must arise from a power far superior to anything human. If so, then the Army is everywhere a standing manifestation of the saving **power of God**, and a standing reproof to the "modern thought" which ignores that power.

The one-minded and one-heartedness of the Army is strikingly exemplified in its newspapers and its prayers. It has twenty-four *War Crys*, published in as many different countries and colonies, in their several languages. In not one of these can there be found any recognition of the controversies which disturb the Christian world! They represent minds always engaged upon the one subject, lives entirely devoted to the one object--the subjugation of the world to the dominion of Jesus Christ. In prayer this absolute union of heart and mind is even more remarkable. In the course of more than twenty years there have of course arisen frequently within the Army differences and disputings, which could not have been easily brought to an end but for the exercise of a strong central authority; but it is a remarkable fact that these differences have scarcely ever arisen from any variety of **opinions**, and in only one or two instances from the introduction of any new teaching. I was very much impressed lately with the Army's oneness in prayer, during a tour in which I had the opportunity to observe closely the action of soldiers of half a dozen different nations in succession. I do not wonder that the Army is reproached with the constant use of a few phrases, repeated over and over again. The accusation is gloriously correct to this extent--that officers and soldiers, to whatever class or nation they may belong, and wherever you may meet them, appear to have their minds so concentrated upon the one great theme, and their whole energies so thoroughly called out for the accomplishment of the one result, that to hear one is to hear all.

Now to what conclusion can one come but that either all this union is produced by one Almighty Spirit working "all in all"--according to the Scriptures, making His real followers not only of one spirit but "of one mind," giving them to "see light in His light," producing in every one the same purpose and the same entire subjection to the will of Christ,--or else that we are in presence of the most astounding wonder of the age, without having placed before us any means of accounting for its existence?

This becomes all the more evident when we look at the **financial** system of the Army. To overcome the general indifference to religion and its teachers, it has become common, in our time, to endeavour to induce the poor to attend the ministrations of this or that religious community by the presentation of gifts, or the provision of gratuitous entertainments. The Salvation Army, on the other hand, goes to the people in every service with its collecting boxes, and pays the rental of expensive buildings everywhere by means of the poor man's pence. Hundreds of thousands of pounds are contributed in this way annually, the people not only meeting the cost of the services conducted in their own immediate neighbourhood, but assisting in the extension of the Army's work all over the world, and showing the greatest readiness to respond to every appeal from new enterprises. There are multitudes of persons whose incomes are between 10*s.* and 20*s.* per week, who give to the Army one or two shillings of that amount, besides devoting so much of their time and strength to its operations, as already explained. The 5,000 officers who have given themselves up entirely to the war, without the guarantee of any salary whatever, merely represent tens of thousands more who would gladly do the same thing, if we were able rapidly enough to arrange for their despatch to every part of the great world-field. We had more than 1,000 such offers in a few weeks of 1887, in England alone. To all these people home and comfort are as enjoyable as to yourself or any one else; yet they glory in the possibility of a while life of self-denying activity for Christ, and eagerly look forward to the day when, far from home and old friends, their bodies shall be lowered into a salvation soldier's grave, amid the tears and prayers of others now revelling in sinful indulgence, but induced by their life, example, and testimony to leave all and follow Christ.

Let no one say in presence of a vast assemblage of facts like this, that it is no longer required of us, or no longer within our power, to follow in the footsteps of the prophets and apostles of the past. Amidst the snows of Lapland, as well as in the Indian jungle, on the outskirts of European occupancy in the far West and the other side of the world, as well as in the midst of crowded European and American cities, men and women are proving every day that the experiences of the Psalms,-- the very experiences of God's presence and salvation, which in apostolic days made the poor, despised, and persecuted followers of the Messiah the happiest of beings,--are now within the reach of all who will equally deny themselves, take up their cross and follow Him who became poor in order to make others rich for ever.

The Salvation Army deserves and demands the careful and patient study of all who would learn how best to follow God and hasten the coming of His kingdom. The more closely and carefully you examine, the more fully will you be driven to the conclusion--the opinions of the day to the contrary, notwithstanding--that those who truly wish to follow Christ at all costs can do so in this age as well as in previous ones, and will succeed, just as others have done before, in gaining the world's hatred, the smile of God, and the victory which He guarantees to all who trust in and obey Him.

INTERNATIONAL HEADQUARTERS OF THE SALVATION ARMY, LONDON, E.C. July, 1887.

Also from Diggory Press

By William Booth

In Darkest England and the Way Out

(ISBN 184685377X)

Purity of Heart

(ISBN 1846853761)

By Catherine Booth

Aggressive Christianity

(ISBN 1905363117)

Hot Saints

(ISBN 18468535152)

Let the Women Speak (Female Teaching)

(ISBN 1846853753)

Printed in the United Kingdom
by Lightning Source UK Ltd.
123916UK00003B/138/A